PELICAN BOOKS
A519

LEONARDO
SIGMUND FREUD

D0415548

SIGMUND FREUD

LEONARDO DA VINCI

AND A MEMORY OF HIS CHILDHOOD

TRANSLATED BY ALAN TYSON
WITH AN INTRODUCTION
BY BRIAN FARRELL

PENGUIN BOOKS

Penguin Books Ltd, Harmondsworth, Middlesex
AUSTRALIA: Penguin Books Pty Ltd, 762 Whitehorse Road,
Mitcham, Victoria

—

Eine Kindheitserinnerung des Leonardo da Vinci first published 1910

This translation, by Alan Tyson, was first published (as *Leonardo da Vinci
and a Memory of his Childhood* in Volume Eleven of the Standard Edition
of the Complete Psychological Works of Sigmund Freud, edited by
James Strachey in collaboration with Anna Freud and assisted by
Alix Strachey and Alan Tyson) by The Hogarth Press and the
Institute of Psycho-Analysis (by arrangement with Routledge and
Kegan Paul) in 1957

—

Published in Pelican Books 1963

—

Introduction Copyright © Brian Farrell, 1963

—

Made and printed in Great Britain
by Cox and Wyman Ltd
London, Reading, and Fakenham
Set in Monotype Baskerville

CONTENTS

Grateful acknowledgement is made to the Phaidon Press for permission to quote in the Introduction from Ludwig Goldscheider's *Leonardo da Vinci*.

INTRODUCTION

I

It is generally agreed that Leonardo da Vinci is a complex and puzzling individual. When we contemplate his life and work we find ourselves struggling to understand him and to dispel the enigma he presents. In this essay, Freud offers us his own attempt to understand Leonardo.

When we are ordinarily puzzled by someone, for example, our new neighbour next door, what puzzles us are the apparent inconsistencies in his life and general conduct. Thus, our new neighbour might say he is very interested in gardening, but he lets his large garden go to ruin; when his luggage came it was seen to contain various pieces of sporting equipment, but he appears to play no sport and hardly goes out at all. We would probably be puzzled by items of this sort. But when we discover that his wife has only just died, that gardening and sport were joint activities of theirs, and that he is still too distressed by her death to take up the normal round again, we then feel we have solved the puzzle – that we now understand him. We succeed therefore in understanding our neighbour when we can produce an explanatory narrative about him which (*a*) removes the apparent inconsistencies and presents a coherent picture of him instead; and (*b*) is true.

Now we are puzzled about Leonardo, at least in part, for the very same reasons that we are perplexed about our neighbour. His life and work present us with glaring inconsistencies. Possessed of prodigious talents in many directions, his actual achievements seem to fall far short of his real capabilities – his inability to finish a piece of work, for instance, was notorious. His painting and drawing is full of feeling but hardly ever in his written records does he exhibit any feeling for any human being whatever. Moreover, his artistic work as a whole presents a mysterious picture to the student. In the words of Sir Kenneth Clark he is 'the Hamlet of art history',[1] and his whole life leaves us uncertain whether he is an artist distracted by his scientific interests or a scientist who also happened to be an artist. In this essay Freud offers us the fruits of his own attempt to understand Leonardo. He tries therefore to give us an explanatory narrative in which the inconsistencies of Leonardo's life and work are removed and the whole exhibited as a coherent story. However, it is not unlikely that Freud's essay will strike many ordinary laymen as an odd and fantastic exercise. Hence it is worth noting and remembering how it does resemble the sort of explanatory narratives we offer about people who puzzle us in ordinary life.

But, of course, there is a critical difference between Freud's essay and the narrative we offered about our new neighbour. In seeking to understand and explain our neighbour, we make use of the psychology of ordinary life – of common sense. Thus we remove the inconsistency between our neighbour's professed interest in gardening and his actual neglect of his garden by showing that the latter is an expected outcome of his bereavement and present very depressed state. However, in attempting to explain Leonardo, Freud does not restrict himself to the psychology of common sense. On the contrary, what Freud is specifically concerned to do is to try to understand him by means of the very technical concepts and generalizations of psycho-

1. Clark, Kenneth. *Leonardo da Vinci*. Harmondsworth (Penguin Books), 1958, p. 159.

analytic theory. In addition to making use of the psychology of common sense wherever necessary, Freud applies to the data we have about Leonardo the technical apparatus of psycho-analytic theory – as far as he and others had developed it at the time. It is this feature that makes Freud's essay quite different logically from a common sense narrative about a person. What is more, it is this feature that also logically distinguishes Freud's essay from the attempts usually made to understand Leonardo by art critics, historians of art, and specialists of this type; for these specialists also rely for the most part on a psychology of common sense to resolve the enigma of Leonardo. No doubt, it is a sophisticated and subtle common sense – somewhat removed from the simple-minded notions and generalizations sufficient to understand our new neighbour. But it nevertheless remains, largely or wholly, a psychology of common sense.

Now when the ordinary person, or the art critic, or the historian of science or art turns to this essay by Freud, he is likely to be interested, puzzled, and disconcerted. He will be interested because he will feel that Freud's narrative is illuminating, that because of it he now understands things about Leonardo that he did not understand before, and so on. But he will also be disconcerted and puzzled because he will not know what to make of it all. How much credence should he attach to Freud's story? What reasons are there to believe that it is true? These doubts about the essay are quite natural and understandable. As we have seen, what distinguishes Freud's essay about Leonardo from the usual run of narratives is that it uses the technical concepts and generalizations of psycho-analytic theory. If these concepts and generalizations had the logical character of, say, the concepts and generalizations of mechanics or the kinetic theory of gases or the theory of genetics, then they would be generally accepted and there would be no problem. All we should have to be sure about was that Freud had applied the concepts and generalizations of psycho-analysis correctly to the particular instance of Leonardo. If the consensus of the scientific world was that Freud had applied them correctly to the data of Leonardo's life and work, the ordinary man and art critic could then rely on this consensus and agree that Freud *had* explained the puzzling phenomena presented by Leonardo. He might be surprised by Freud's explanatory narrative; but then surprise is characteristic of scientific explanation. He might not even grasp it himself, but again failure by laymen to grasp an explanation is frequent in science. What there would be no room for would be any doubts and perplexities about Freud's account itself. But, of course, we all know that the concepts and generalizations of psycho-analysis have a logical character that makes them very different from the concepts and generalizations of mechanics or genetics. Because of these differences there is at present no consensus in the scientific world about the concepts and generalizations of psycho-analysis. Some thinkers, indeed, even maintain that psycho-analysis is not a scientific enterprise at all. So the ordinary person or the student of art is unable to fall back on a consensus of scientific opinion about psycho-analysis, and therefore about this essay by Freud. The scientific world gives him no guidance on the question. When he reads the essay he finds in it a technical psychology whose validity he cannot personally assess. He finds that this psychology is being applied to a particular historical figure, and that he is unable to determine for himself how legitimate the application is. Naturally, therefore, he is bewildered by Freud's essay.

Naturally, he wonders how much credence to attach to it. Is Freud's story about Leonardo just a typical piece of psycho-analytic phantasy? Or is there something in it? And if so, how much?

2

Let us begin by outlining the argument that Freud offers us. His narrative focuses our attention on an early memory of Leonardo about a bird. Unfortunately there is an immediate difficulty about this memory that we must clear out of the way. At the beginning of Chapter Two of the essay, Freud writes as follows:

There is, so far as I know, only one place in his scientific notebooks where Leonardo inserts a piece of information about his childhood. In a passage about the flight of vultures he suddenly interrupts himself to pursue a memory from very early years which had sprung to his mind: 'It seems that I was always destined to be so deeply concerned with vultures; for I recall as one of my very earliest memories that while I was in my cradle a vulture came down to me, and opened my mouth with its tail, and struck me many times with its tail against my lips'.

This quotation from Leonardo[1] is the English version

[1]. Codice Atlantico, 66 v. This is usually written: C.A. 66 v. (on page 118 of this edition) Freud gives the reference inaccurately as '65 v'.) In subsequent references to Leonardo's words the following abbreviations will also be used:

Q = Quaderni Anatomia,

H = an MS. in the Library of the Institut de France.

SKM = Codices Foster in the library of the Victoria and Albert Museum.

The student can consult Leonardo's writings in J. P. Richter *The Literary Works of Leonardo da Vinci*, compiled and edited from the original manuscripts (rev. ed., 2 vols., London, 1939). For a selection from the writings, see Edward McCurdy, *Leonardo da Vinci's Note-Books*, London (Duckworth), 1906; and Irma A. Richter, *Selections from the Notebooks of Leonardo da Vinci*, London, (O.U.P.), 1952.

of the German translation that Freud used. Unfortunately the German translation from the Italian is defective in two places – as the editor of *The Standard Edition* of Freud's works points out.[1] First, the Italian original ends with the words '*dentro alle labbra*'. In the German translation the word '*dentro*', meaning 'within', is omitted. Freud, however, seems to have noticed this and interpreted the original Italian text correctly. The second defect is a serious one. The German translation translates the Italian word '*nibbio*' as '*Geier*', which means vulture. This is a mistake. '*Nibbio*' is the word for 'kite'.[2] In this passage Leonardo is talking about kites, not vultures. This mistake of translation has misled Freud and others to some extent. Accordingly, certain parts of his original narrative – parts which are easy to pick out – have to be rejected outright; and his explanation correspondingly modified. Let us suppose, then, that Freud had understood Leonardo correctly to be referring to kites; and let us examine Freud's explanation in the modified form it would then take.

Freud argues that this report of Leonardo resembles the memory phantasies about early childhood produced by patients in the course of being psycho-analysed. Now the report of such a phantasy is a report of an event that never happened. But the patient produces it in the form that he does because, roughly, he has an unconscious adult wish which fixes on some past and related experience of the person when a child, and which now transforms this experience in a way that permits the open but disguised expression of his unconscious wish. Therefore, in producing this phantasy report, Leonardo reveals that an unconscious adult wish is at work in him. What is this wish? Freud claims that Leonardo's

1. See pp. 8–9.
2. Leonardo spelt the word 'nibbio' with one 'b'.

report about the kite is yet another instance of a well-known type of phantasy, which patients under analysis have shown to have a clear-cut and well-established significance. Leonardo places his story back in the period when he was in his cradle and still at the breast. Therefore it contains 'a reminiscence of sucking – or being suckled – at his mother's breast'. This is the past experience that his phantasy has fixed on and transformed. In telling us this story about the kite in his cradle, Leonardo reveals that he has transformed the experience of sucking the breast into one in which a kite opens his mouth and beats about inside it with its tail. In telling us this he reveals that he has an unconscious concern with 'the idea of an act of fellatio, a sexual act in which the penis is put into the mouth of the person involved'. So Leonardo's story reveals an unconscious wish typical of a passive homosexual, namely, to commit the act of fellatio. The early experience of sucking the breast has been transformed into the report about a kite – the phantasy of a passive homosexual – thereby permitting the open but disguised expression of his homosexuality and his unconscious wish to suck a penis.

But why does Leonardo substitute a kite for his mother? How does the penis, which is the essence of the male, come to take the place of the breast, which is so essentially female and maternal? Why is it that the early experience of the act of sucking at the breast has been transformed by Leonardo into one in which the kite is active and he is inactive? Where have the elements of *passive* homosexuality come from? Because of the mistake in translation already mentioned, Freud was misled into trying to answer the question 'Why does Leonardo substitute a vulture for his mother?'; and his answer to his question does not apply to the kite. Hence, the essay does not tell us why a kite takes the place of his mother. The essay answers the second question (How does the penis come to take the place of the breast?) by resorting to Freud's doctrine about infantile theories of sexuality. A small boy believes that his mother also has a penis. His erotic interest in his mother culminates in a longing for her penis, and in the course of his development he may develop a fixation on this object – a fixation that is pathologically manifested in foot-fetishists, in '*coupeurs de nattes*', and so forth. Therefore, Leonardo's emphasis on the tale of a kite is a way of telling us that there was a time when he was curious about his mother and believed she had a genital like his own. But where does the passivity and homosexuality come from? Psycho-analytical experience has shown that, with one type of male homosexual, the patients have all had as small children a very intense erotic attachment to a female, usually the mother. 'This attachment', Freud writes,

was evoked or encouraged by too much tenderness on the part of the mother herself, and further reinforced by the small part played by the father during their childhood.

But the growing boy is finally forced to repress his love for the mother and he does this in these circumstances by identifying himself with her. The boy is now protected against his love for her, because he now plays the role of mother himself and chooses persons like himself as his love objects. Hence his homosexuality. Freud suggests that this is the fate that overcame Leonardo. When very young, his mother was over-affectionate and his father played a small role in his life. When Leonardo refers in the kite phantasy to the tail striking him many time against the lips, he is referring, not only to the experience of sucking, but also to the experience or memory in which 'my mother pressed innumerable passionate kisses on my mouth'. Hence, the passive character of the kite phantasy. In it he is expressing the adult wish to play the passive partner in a homosexual act of sucking a penis.

Freud's interpretation of the kite memory is only part, however, of something much more important – namely, his whole attempt to reconstruct the personality of Leonardo. Freud draws attention to what were at the time the known facts about Leonardo's early life; and he notes the following in particular: that Leonardo was an illegitimate child of a woman called Caterina; that he is listed, when five years old, as being among the members of his father's household; that his father married a certain Donna Albiera, and that this marriage was childless; that he later entered Verrocchio's studio as an apprentice; and that at the age of twenty his name appears as a member of the Painters' Guild in Florence.

Freud now offers a hypothetical account of Leonardo's early years which he claims is consistent with these facts. He suggests that his father left Leonardo to be brought up by his mother Caterina in her home. Caterina was over-tender with Leonardo and over-eroticized her relations with him – as the kite memory shows. Somewhere between the age of three and five, Leonardo's tie with his mother was broken. He was returned to his father's household and to the care of a young and childless wife. About this same stage Leonardo had to repress his sexual interest in, and curiosity about, his mother Caterina. This is the normal thing that happens at this time. Because of his close erotic attachment to Caterina, he achieved this repression by identifying himself with her and thereby forcing himself to choose love objects like himself, as we have already seen. But in Leonardo's case the repression of sex interest was severe. No doubt this was due in part to the shattering effect on him of the rupture from the mother who meant so much to him. But it was also due in part to factors in Leonardo's biological make-up about which psycho-analysis cannot speak, and about which in any case nothing is yet known. The effect of this severe repression, however, was to make him sublimate much of his sexual energy and interests into curiosity and a craving for knowledge. So Leonardo entered adolescence with his sexual impulse homosexually directed, but most of it sublimated into his craving for knowledge. The upshot was to reduce his sexual need very greatly, and so make it unlikely that the homosexual bent given to it would lead him into sexual behaviour. In addition, Freud reminds us, 'What an artist creates provides at the same time an outlet for his sexual desire.' Accordingly, in taking to artistic work Leonardo solved the problem of his adolescence by discharging in this work the upsurging sexual energies of this stage of his life. All this provided a fairly satisfactory solution at the time of his psychological problem. In particular, this solution enabled him to follow the lead of his genius in the fine arts and to use his talents in this field without inhibition at the outset of his career.

Freud points to certain known facts about Leonardo that lend independent support to part of this reconstruction of his personality, namely, the part concerned with his homosexuality. Freud notes the absence of any woman with whom he had any intimacy, physical or mental; as a teacher he surrounded himself with handsome boys and youths; and, whether rightly or wrongly, he was accused and acquitted of homosexual practices when still an apprentice. He was clearly an aesthete and had a love of the refinements of living. His strong repression of ordinary sexuality comes out in one

place in his writings where he records his disgust at the
whole act of procreation, as he does also in his drawing
of coitus. Freud also points to the chaste character of his
writings as a whole, and the absence of the obscene
drawings one expects among the private papers of
artists. 'In an age', he writes, 'which saw a struggle between sensuality without restraint and gloomy asceticism,
ism, Leonardo represented the cool repudiation of
sexuality.'

3

With the help of this reconstruction of Leonardo's
personality, Freud attempts to remove the inconsistencies in his life and work and so makes him understandable. As we have noted, Freud argues that Leonardo
achieved a relatively satisfactory solution of his problem
in the course of his adolescence. Consequently in his
youth he passed through a period of vigorous artistic
creation, in which he worked without obvious inhibition. But it is a psycho-analytic discovery that 'the
almost total repression of a real sexual life does not
provide the most favourable conditions for the exercise
of sublimated sexual trends'. The sexual needs that
Leonardo is denying begin to break through. The first
thing to happen is that the later, and second, sublimation of his energies into art begins to break down. He
finds himself incapable of vigorous and decisive artistic
work. He finds himself delaying, hesitating, and becoming incapable of completing anything. A striking example is his work on 'The Last Supper'. Now all this
is like the process of regression that neurotics exhibit.
So it is evident that Leonardo regressed from the later
position, in which his sublimated energies found their
outlet in his art, to the earlier position, in which they

were sublimated into the craving for knowledge. At first, Freud reminds us, this interest was still in the service of his art. But as he did not solve his own psychological problem, the regression became permanent and fully developed. His craving for knowledge came to dominate his work, and to develop independently and away from his art. Hence the Janus-like character of Leonardo, part artist, part scientist, and his development from the former into the latter.

Next, let us remember, his father had left him to be brought up by Caterina. Freud supposes that this fact also had an important and shattering effect on the young child in yet another way. It made him come unconsciously to regard his father as a person who had neglected him when a child, who had not cared about him, and who had left him as an undeveloped infant to the sole charge of his mother. Later on in his childhood, Leonardo identified himself with his father in the usual manner. In doing so, he came unconsciously to adopt the same attitude as his father to his own offspring, that is, to the products of his own work. He did not particularly care about them. He found it difficult to sustain his interest in them. He could not bother to finish them, and to see that they were properly developed and completed. Now this early unconscious attitude also played its part in breaking down his adolescent solution of his difficulties. For it helped, along with his regression to the desire for knowledge, to make him indifferent to the fate of his painting and artistic work; and, what is more serious, made it difficult for him to bring *any* of his work to fruition. Hence, also, the unfinished, doodling character of his scientific work. Freud does not actually discuss the influence on his scientific activity of Leonardo's identification with his father. But the suggestion just made is quite consistent with Freud's own narrative; and some such suggestion is necessary if Freud is also to explain the unfinished nature of Leonardo's scientific work.

Freud also attempts to explain some of the content of Leonardo's scientific work and outlook. Leonardo had learnt in his first five years to do without his father's support, and to pursue his sexual researches without his interference. This prepared him later, on reaching maturity, to reject parental and parent-like figures and authority. So he was able to reject the appeal to authority and the ancients, and become the first natural scientist. Likewise, he was able to reject the Christian view of a personal god, as he had no need of an exalted father figure, and was thus able to detach himself from Christian orthodoxy. Leonardo's rejection of authority 'simply corresponds to', or symbolizes, his rejection of his father; and Freud implies that the same is true of his rejection of Christianity. Freud notes that a wish to fly in dreams turns out under psycho-analysis to be a longing to be capable of sexual performance. This longing, says Freud, is an early infantile wish. Leonardo's early sexual interests in his mother were frustrated, broken off and then severely repressed. What is worse, he could only deal with the problem of his mother's excessive over-tenderness by adopting a homosexual solution, as we have already seen, thereby incapacitating himself from having ordinary sexual intercourse. Now we know that Leonardo was fascinated by the problems of flight. We can understand this when we regard his interest in this whole subject as a displaced manifestation of his repressed sexuality. His longing to solve the problem of flight and to fly was an expression of his unconscious wish for the sexual performance of which he was incapable.

But what about the content of Leonardo's work as an

artist? How does Freud try to explain the special and peculiar character of Leonardo's art? A quick perusal of the essay is enough to show that Freud only attempts to deal with certain features of Leonardo's paintings which he says are puzzling. For this limited purpose he concentrates on two paintings – the 'Mona Lisa' and the 'Madonna and Child with St Anne'.

Freud makes the supposition that at the age of fifty Leonardo underwent a further development characteristic of middle-age. His sexual impulse 'made a further energetic advance'. He regressed to a still earlier phase of development, and 'still deeper layers of the contents of his mind became active once more'. It was at this period that he met and painted Mona Lisa del Giocondo. Freud now cuts through the perennial enigma of the 'Mona Lisa' at one stroke. He supposes that, with the deeper layers of Leonardo's mind already stirring, this Florentine woman 'awakened in him as a grown man the memory of the mother of his early childhood', and in her smile he saw 'his mother's happy smile of sensual rapture'. The painting at once becomes understandable. The expression of the face is a perfect representation, Freud reminds us, of 'the contrasts which dominate the erotic life of women; the contrast between reserve and seduction, and between the most devoted tenderness and a sensuality that is ruthlessly demanding – consuming men as if they were alien beings'. But these contrasts represent precisely how Leonardo was treated by his mother. She over-eroticized her relations with him. In so doing she treated him with tenderness and yet with a sensuality which ended by robbing him of his masculinity. Hence the smile of inner satisfaction and menace, the smile of the cat that has eaten the canary. We know that Leonardo was obviously involved in, and obsessed by, this painting for years. Naturally so, as he was painting one who unconsciously represented a mother from whom he had never really escaped. Leonardo clearly became obsessed by the smile, since it appeared from that date in all his later work. Naturally so, in view of its critical significance for him in his whole life and work.

A little later on Leonardo painted 'The Madonna and Child with St Anne'. This painting is puzzling, Freud says, because it represents a subject rarely handled in Italian painting, and because St Anne is presented as a young woman of radiant beauty. The puzzle vanishes if we make use of one of Freud's suppositions about Leonardo's childhood. Freud supposed that he was first brought up by Caterina for some years, and then cared for by the young Donna Albiera, the childless wife of his father. The significance of the picture is that it 'contains a synthesis of the history of his childhood'. It represents for Leonardo his own childhood – two young mothers of about the same age watching over and caring for him, each endowed with the typical Leonardesque smile. The still later pictures, such as the 'St John', reveal somewhat different features. They still have the familiar smile but they also 'breathe a mystical air into whose secret one dare not penetrate'; and they portray androgynous figures – beautiful youths of feminine delicacy and form – who 'gaze in mysterious triumph as if they knew of a great achievement of happiness about which silence must be kept'. Freud suggests that these figures represent a psychological triumph for Leonardo. Denied of an erotic life, he has represented in these figures the wishes of a boy who was infatuated with his mother. He has fulfilled these wishes by presenting the male and female natures in these figures as blissfully united; and the familiar smile shows us that the secret and mysterious triumph is that of love.

4

What are we to make of this explanatory narrative?

The first thing is to note where Freud was, or may have been, wrong about certain matters of fact. Since Freud wrote, evidence has come to light, which suggests that Leonardo was brought up in his father's household with Albiera from an early age.[1] This suggestion may make it necessary to modify Freud's narrative. If we suppose that Leonardo was at least breast-fed by Caterina and only left her towards the end of, say, his first year of life, then we would be able, perhaps, to keep the main outlines of Freud's account and merely modify it by supposing that the eroticizing by, and identification with, the mother took place at a much earlier age. Given the general looseness of Freudian theory, such a modification would be quite feasible, and, moreover, in line with current psycho-analytic thinking, which places some of the critical phases of development at much earlier ages than Freud himself suggested. If, however, we suppose that Leonardo was not breast-fed by Caterina but placed at once in the care of Albiera, then it would be more difficult perhaps to keep the main outlines of Freud's own narrative. Psycho-analysts might then be forced into giving quite a different account of Leonardo from that of Freud – one in which the schizoid and depressive features of his personality played a central role. Another possible mistake is this. Freud seriously imagines (in Chapter Three) that the Caterina mentioned in Leonardo's notebooks, and whose burial expenses he records, was his mother. Most contemporary historians seem to think that there is nothing to support this idea. If an analyst wishes to explain the records of the burial expenses,

1. Möller, Emil. 'Der Geburtstag des Lionardo da Vinci', *Jahrbuch der preussischen Kunstsammlungen*, 60 (1939), 71–5.

he would be advised to do so in some other way.[1]

Freud makes a different sort of mistake about Leonardo's drawing of coition. In the 1919 edition of his essay he adds in a long footnote part of an article by an analyst called Reitler, including a coition figure said to have been drawn by Leonardo (see pp. 100–3). It is clear that Freud is in general agreement with the tenor of this quotation. Now Reitler's article is based on the reproduction of this coition figure, and the only drawing in Leonardo's corpus which this can represent is on Q III 3 v. (p. 103). But the reproduction of this coition figure from Q III 3 v. is wrong – both in Reitler's original article and in *The Standard Edition* of Freud's essay used in this volume. It is wrong in two respects. It presents the two feet – one of the man's and one of the woman's – as complete; in the actual drawing Leonardo does not complete the legs and feet at all. In this reproduction the expression is such that Reitler can describe it as follows:

The features of the man ... are marked by a resistance which is positively indignant. His brows are wrinkled and his gaze is directed sideways with an expression of repugnance. The lips are pressed together and their corners are then drawn down.

This face, he concludes, 'expresses only indignation and aversion'. In the actual drawing, however, the brows are not wrinkled, the gaze is not directed sideways, the lips are not pressed together, and their corners then drawn down. In consequence the whole expression is quite

1. Thus, Freud supports his argument by one text (p. 146*n*. below) which is incorrect. It should read: 'Giovannina has a fantastic face, lives at Santa Caterina, at the hospital.' (SKM II 3r; I. Richter, op. cit., p. 322; and J. P. Richter, op cit., Vol. II, p. 352). Clearly this does not refer to the woman Caterina. Further, the burial expenses are given by J. P. Richter in soldi, not florins (op. cit., Vol. II, p. 379, 1522).

different. It is, if anything, one of peaceful bliss, or calmness, or 'strange detachment' – to use Sir Kenneth Clark's words.[1] We need not stay to discuss the origin of this mistake.[2] Freud uses this drawing as an additional

1. Clark, Kenneth, op. cit., p. 143.

2. The history of the mistake seems to be as follows. The original drawing is on Q III 3 v. (see p. 103 of this edition; a collotype reproduction appears in the definitive edition of the *Quaderni d'Anatomia* by Ove C. L. Vangensten, A. Fonahn, and H. Hopstock, 6 vols., Christiania, 1911–16). This was reproduced, in an engraving by Bartolozzi, in Chamberlain's *Royal Collection of Drawings*, 1812. This reproduction was inaccurate. Bartolozzi put in the feet, and put them in wrongly; he shaded in the eye; and he introduced lines on the forehead and on the side of the mouth. But he left the general expression of the face detached or reposeful. Next came a volume whose shortened title and reference reads: *Tabula Anatomica Leonardo da Vinci*, Lunaeburgi, 1830. This volume contains a lithograph by Wehrt, which purports to be a reproduction of the original drawing, Q III 3 v. Now there is no evidence that Wehrt ever had access to the original; and when one places his lithograph alongside Bartolozzi's engraving, it is clear on inspection that the former is a copy of the latter – Wehrt obtained the lithograph by copying Bartolozzi. This is clear not only from a study of the coition figure, but also from a study of the other drawings and the handwriting on the same sheet. In making his copy Wehrt incorporated the errors that Bartolozzi had already committed, and added others of his own. In particular, he so changed the face as to give it the expression that appears in the Freud–Reitler reproduction. The next step in the history appears to have been a work by Eduard Fuchs with the following title and reference: *Illustrierte Sittengeschichte vom Mittelalter bis zur Gegenwart.* Renaissance, Ergänzungsband. Privatdruck, Albert Langen, München (Date of Preface: 1909). This book reproduces the coition figure as it appears in Wehrt's lithograph; and it is this book that Reitler gives as his source of Leonardo's drawing in his article ('Eine anatomisch-künstlerische Fehlleistung Leonardos da Vinci', *Int. Z. Psychoan.*, 4, 205). The history of the Freud–Reitler mistake becomes patent to the eye when one places the three reproductions alongside one another in order of date – the original drawing, in the collotype of Vangensten *et al.*, the Bartolozzi engraving, and the lithograph by Wehrt.

item of evidence to support his view that Leonardo had repudiated sexuality, and it is clear that Freud cannot place any weight on it. Moreover, the 'remarkable errors' that Freud says are also visible in this drawing can be given another and historical interpretation, which we shall touch on below.

5

Let us, however, ignore Freud's possible and actual mistakes of fact. The next thing to note is that in certain ways Freud's narrative lays itself open to the charge of being quite inadequate and even silly.

(*a*) In two brief passages Freud refers to Leonardo's difficulties as being akin to those of an obsessional neurotic. But Freud leaves it quite unclear how this alleged obsessionalism took its rise, and how it is related to the development and fate of his sexual impulse. Moreover, it is far from clear how large or small a part of Leonardo's conduct his alleged obsessionalism is meant to explain, and how important this part is supposed to be. One seems bound to conclude that Freud did not think out carefully his references to Leonardo's obsessionalism and relate them adequately to the rest of his narrative.

(*b*) We have noted how Freud attempts to explain Leonardo's interest in flying as an expression of his unconscious wish for sexual performance. Now let us suppose that Freud's whole theory of sexuality is correct. It is quite clear that Freud's account of Leonardo's interest in flying is not *sufficient* to explain it. For *all* Freud claims is that this interest has its 'roots' in Leonardo's early sexual life – that it is a displaced expression of his repressed sexuality and of his unconscious longing for sexual performance. Freud does not say how this interest developed out of his unconscious wishes – why his repressed sexuality was displaced into an interest in flying, rather than into something else. But as the repression of sexuality is common to all of us on Freud's view, it is evident that Freud is not saying much. The important and interesting thing to know about Leonardo would be the conditions that made his repressed sexuality come out in the displaced form of an interest in flying; and Freud has no explanation to offer of this. At most, therefore, Freud is telling us that an unconscious longing by Leonardo for sexual performance is a *necessary* condition of his interest in flight. But how much does this amount to? It would be a very important contention if this unconscious longing were a necessary condition for an interest in flight *alone*. But Freud does not make this claim, and the perusal of psycho-analytic literature makes it evident that the unconscious wish for sexual performance serves as a necessary condition for all sorts of interests, activities, and personal difficulties. Hence Freud is telling us something which is more trivial and uninteresting than might appear at first sight. Taken by itself, Freud's whole explanation here seems grossly inadequate and lays itself open to the charge of being silly and futile.

(*c*) Freud's attempt to account for Leonardo's rejection of traditional Christianity runs into similar objections. So, too, does his attempt to explain the origin of Leonardo's craving for knowledge and interest in science. It is obviously not sufficient to explain Leonardo's craving as the sublimated outcome of repressing his sexual interest in, and curiosity about, his mother. For, according to Freud, such repression is a normal thing that happens, and yet we do not all develop a craving for knowledge as the result. Nor is it sufficient to explain his craving as the outcome of the *severe* repression of sexual interests, to which Leonardo was subjected on Freud's supposition. This will not do because different people react differently to severe repression, as Freud points out. We want to know why Leonardo reacted as he did; and Freud does not tell us. At best, therefore, Freud is saying that the severe repression of sexual curiosity and interest which Leonardo underwent provided a necessary condition for the development of his craving for knowledge, and so, later on, for his regression into science. But even this limited contention runs into the same objection of relative triviality which, we saw, can be levelled at Freud's explanation of his interest in flight. For, it could be argued, patients under analysis show that the severe repression of sexual curiosity is a necessary condition for all sorts of activities and interests, other than a craving for knowledge. Consequently, in telling us that this is a necessary condition with Leonardo for his interest in science, Freud is really telling us very little indeed.

But this conclusion leaves us uneasy; it seems so exaggerated. Many years ago Professor Broad criticized the 'pretentious futility' that, he alleged, was 'typical of some of the sillier psycho-analysts', which would 'explain' a taste for music as due to repressed sexual desire.[1] In our discussion so far we seem to have convicted Freud of this very pretentious futility that Professor Broad objected to. But we hesitate about accepting this conclusion, because Freud is clearly getting at *something* in his examination of Leonardo's interest in flight and science. He is not just being pretentious and futile. What, then, is he getting at? What is the source of our uneasiness?

1. Broad, C. D. *The Mind and its Place in Nature*, Ch. I. London (Kegan Paul), 1925.

Let us notice that there are two different ways of describing what Freud is doing at this point. We can say that he is trying to give an explanation of, for example, Leonardo's interest in flight and science, which is of the same sort as that provided in the natural sciences. Freud himself seems to have accepted as correct this description of what he was doing. Now when an event is fully explained to us in natural science, it will be found that we have also been given the necessary and sufficient conditions for the occurrence of the event. This is a large and important piece of information. It is quite clear, however, that Freud does not give us the sufficient conditions of Leonardo's interest in flight and science, and only draws attention to a necessary condition that tells us very little. If, therefore, we say that Freud is explaining Leonardo's interest in the way that is done in natural science, we convict him of utter inadequacy, and we expose his explanations as perfect examples of pretentious futility. But because Freud is obviously getting at *something* here, it follows that this description is misleading. It is not right to say that he is just doing a piece of natural science. Once we do say this, we develop the wrong expectations about the essay, and then inevitably convict him of inadequacy.

However, there is another different way of describing what he is doing. We can use the description suggested at the outset and say that Freud is trying to provide a coherent story about Leonardo which removes the inconsistencies in his life and work, and which is true. On this second description, what Freud is primarily concerned to do is to fit together the known facts about Leonardo with the aid of the technical generalizations and concepts of psycho-analysis. Now the known facts may be too sparse, and/or psycho-analytic theory too limited in its scope to enable Freud to provide a narrative which will answer *all* the questions about Leonardo that we should like Freud to deal with. Hence he may not be able to give us a narrative which embodies, for example, the necessary and sufficient conditions of Leonardo's interest in flight and science. But the fact that he cannot do this may not matter much on the second description of his activity. For on this second account of it, all Freud has to do is to fit together this interest of Leonardo with the rest of the data we have about him. He has to show that these are mutually consistent and supporting. Now let us suppose that Leonardo had revealed (*a*) an intense interest in flight and science which looked very much like a symptom of regression; and (*b*) no evidence that his sexual impulses were severely repressed, but, on the contrary, evidence that they were fully and adequately realized and exercised. It would then have been a little difficult for Freud to fit together these two facts about Leonardo. For, on psycho-analytic theory, a regressive interest in flight and science is typically a manifestation of an unconscious wish for sexual performance, and related wishes; and this presupposes that, where such regressive interests are shown, the sexual impulse has undergone considerable or severe repression. Accordingly, it is necessary and important for Freud to show that Leonardo's regressive interest does go along with considerable or severe repression. This is what psycho-analytic theory leads us to expect, and Freud tries to show that this expectation is realized with Leonardo. Thus, he points out, in effect, how the supposition that Leonardo's sexual impulse was subjected to severe repression is supported by all sorts of things in the data, other than his interest in flight and science. This fact indirectly supports Freud's suggestion that Leonardo's interest in flight and science was regressive and a symptom of sexual wishes. Again, Freud points, in effect, to the way in which the data lend this latter suggestion independent support. This fact, in turn, gives added weight to the supposition that Leonardo's sexual impulse was severely repressed. So Freud does succeed in showing that Leonardo's interest in flight and science and the other data we have about him are mutually consistent and supporting. Freud is not really concerned to give us a complete account of the way Leonardo's interest developed out of the severe repression of his sexual impulse and his later sexual difficulties. The fact, therefore, that Freud does not give us the necessary and sufficient conditions of Leonardo's interest does not, in itself, count against the point or adequacy of his story. This gap in his story may not matter much, if at all.

In this way, then, we can save Freud's remarks about Leonardo's interest in flight and science from the charge of silliness and pretentious futility. We save them by making clear that Freud is only explaining Leonardo's interest by providing a coherent story about it; he is not trying to explain it in the sort of way characteristic of natural science. But, of course, we can only save this part of Freud's story at a cost. The cost is that we make his remarks at this point much less important than Freud himself, perhaps, thought they were, and much less impressive than they may seem at first sight to the ordinary, unsuspecting reader. The reason for this is clear. Freud may succeed in giving us a coherent story about Leonardo's interest in flight and so forth, and yet tell us very little indeed about Leonardo. The extent to which Freud's story is genuinely informative and impressive depends largely on the degree to which, in giving us a coherent tale, it also succeeds in giving us the necessary and sufficient conditions of Leonardo's interests. Clearly Freud's story does tell us something about these conditions. But our scientific knowledge of human development and pathology is still very incomplete. Likewise, our knowledge about the particular circumstances and details of Leonardo's development and pathology is very defective. Consequently no coherent tale about Leonardo at the present time – whether Freud's or anyone else's – can tell us much about the necessary and sufficient conditions of his interest in flight and science. Freud's remarks about this interest serve to reveal the extent of our present ignorance and an important limitation of his own narrative.

6

We can now come closer to the heart of the problem. If Freud's essay is an attempt to provide a narrative which gives a coherent picture or story of Leonardo's life and work, and in which the inconsistencies in it disappear, are there any reasons that make it obligatory for us to accept Freud's narrative rather than some other? Freud himself noted, in effect, that this question could be asked; for he says that his essay has provoked the criticism that he has merely written a 'psycho-analytic novel'. But he does not do much, if anything, himself to answer this question and meet this criticism.

Now a historian of art may be strongly tempted to assert that a psycho-analytic novel is precisely what Freud has written – at least about topics such as the kite memory, the 'St Anne', and the 'Mona Lisa'. We are not at all obliged, he may argue, to accept Freud's narrative on these topics, because we can explain the oddity of the kite memory and the peculiar features of the 'St Anne' and the 'Mona Lisa' in another way. We can explain them in the way we ordinarily deal with puzzling items in history. We can remove their inconsistencies by putting them back into their historical context with the help of the psychology of common sense. Resort to the technical apparatus of psychoanalysis is quite unnecessary.

Consider the kite memory.[1] Leonardo's reference to this occurs in a context where he is considering the flight of birds, and the kite is picked out because it is the bird in which one can best observe the mechanics of flight, and in particular the movements of its tail. Leonardo probably got the idea of a kite's tail as a rudder from Pliny's *Natural History*, which he knew and quotes. Further, there was a well-known type of story current at that time about an incident in childhood being an omen of adult fortune or genius – for example, how bees settled on Plato's lips which meant that he would have sweetness of speech. In any case, the connexion of a bird with genius or inspiration was very old, and the mouth was a region significant for wisdom and prophecy. In the Christian tradition, for example, the Trinity was often represented in the Middle Ages with a dove's tail in God's mouth; and in Leonardo's time there was a variant in which the wings of the descending bird reached from the lips of God to those of the Son. It is clear, therefore, that Leonardo's kite memory has nothing odd about it. It is a reconstruction of his own past experience suggested by a current tradition and springing from wishes to be destined for greatness and to become great.

1. The argument which follows is largely a summary of the case made about the whole essay by Meyer Schapiro (1956), 'Leonardo and Freud: an Art-Historical Study', *Journal of the History of Ideas*, vol. xvii, 17, no. 2, 147–78.

The position is even clearer about the 'St Anne'. Freud says that this is a puzzling picture because it represents a subject rarely handled in Italian painting and because St Anne is presented as a young and beautiful woman. In fact Freud was mistaken on both points. There had been a widespread and long-standing cult of St Anne and this reached its height in the latter part of the fifteenth century and the beginning of the sixteenth. Anne, Mary, and the Child were worshipped as a more accessible Trinity; and the cult had theological ramifications. Indulgence prayers to St Anne and Mary were issued on sheets with a woodcut of the three; and pictures of them were produced in great numbers – often showing Mary sitting on the lap of St Anne and with the Child on the lap of Mary, an object of tender attentions by both. Furthermore, Anne and Mary had been represented together as young saints long before Leonardo's time. The youth of St Anne is the result of theological idealization, and of the general tendency in medieval and Renaissance art to picture female saints as beautiful and virginal figures. Consequently, as the St Anne is not puzzling in the way that Freud alleged it to be, we do not need to resort to a psycho-analytical story to remove the puzzle.

Freud was also mistaken about the Leonardesque smile. He claims that this dated from the Mona Lisa. In fact the smile appears in what is known as the London cartoon of the St Anne which was drawn in 1500 – before he met Mona Lisa. We also see the smile, or something akin to it, in the smiling faces of Verrocchio, and in plaster sculptures of women and men which – it has been claimed – were among Leonardo's earliest works. The smile also appears in Florentine art long before Leonardo. A present-day scholar has the following remark to make about the Gioconda.

A Frenchman (Robert de Sizeranne, 1896) has observed that Gioconda smiles with only the left part of her mouth – but this is in accordance with the advice given to women in Renaissance times as to how to look most graceful; we read in Agnolo Firenzuola's *Della perfetta bellezza d'una donna*, 1541: 'From time to time, to close the mouth at the right corner with a suave and nimble movement, and to open it at the left side, as if you were smiling secretly . . . not in an artificial manner, but as though unconsciously – this is not affectation, if it is done in moderation and in a restrained and graceful manner and accompanied by innocent coquetry and by certain movements of the eyes. . . .' This is a precept for ladies of fashion, and we should not overlook the fact that Mona Lisa – who plucked her eyebrows and the hair above her brow – was one of them.[1]

All this suggests that the elaborate fuss Freud makes about the smile of the Mona Lisa is quite unnecessary. We can understand it by putting it in its context and recognizing the obvious truth that it owes its power and charm to the infinite delicacy and subtlety of Leonardo's art.

Let us assume that this criticism from the historian is correct on matters of fact. What is its logical force? If Freud, in his narrative about the kite memory, had claimed that the *sole* or *only* origins of this memory were to be found in the circumstances of Leonardo's childhood, then the criticism from the historian would be incompatible with Freud's narrative; and if it were true, Freud's narrative would be false. But Freud does not make this claim. This becomes clear as soon as one pierces the ambiguities of his narrative here and sees it in the context of his writings and work. What Freud was concerned to do was to point to originating conditions that lie in the early history of the person, and to emphasize their importance. He accepted, and indeed

1. Goldscheider, Ludwig. *Leonardo da Vinci*. London (Phaidon Press), 1959, p. 157.

stressed the contribution of subsequent precipitating conditions and of cultural factors in mental functioning. Likewise, if the historian were to claim that the *sole* or *only* origins of this memory are to be found in the literary and scientific traditions of the time, his criticism would be incompatible with Freud's account; and if his criticism were correct, Freud's narrative would be false. But the historian does not claim this either. He merely claims in his criticism of Freud that the kite memory had certain origins in the culture of the time. This view is quite compatible with Freud's hypothesis that the memory had certain origins in Leonardo's relations as a child with his mother. Indeed, it could be argued that the two positions complement each other.

Similarly for the 'St Anne'. Granted that Freud was wrong in the reasons he gave for thinking that the 'St Anne' is a puzzling picture, it is still possible that this picture may have had the psychological significance for Leonardo that Freud maintains. In addition to the religious and contemporary origins of the picture, it may also have had sources in Leonardo's inner and past life that Freud suggested. About the 'Mona Lisa', on the other hand, it is clear that, if we accept that the London cartoon of 'St Anne' and other earlier works contain the Leonardesque smile, we shall have to modify Freud's story. We shall have to say that, though the smile broke out on earlier occasions, it only came to assume critical significance for him about the time of his crisis of middle-age; and with and after the painting of Mona Lisa, it dominated him. However, apart from some such modification, Freud's story about the Mona Lisa remains intact. The fact that the smile has sources in the artistic and social life of the time is quite compatible with it also having the personal sources that Freud has suggested.

But, we may feel like protesting, this is surely a misleading conclusion. Though the historian's account of Leonardo's two paintings and the kite memory does not refute Freud's story about them, surely it does show that his story is *wholly unnecessary*, and hence that there is no obligation on us whatever to adopt it. We may feel like making this protest, because we may be inclined to adopt the general view that, when a personal aberration, or puzzling item in human life, can be explained by common sense or some other rational story, recourse to unconscious motives and the other technical apparatus of psycho-analysis is wholly unnecessary and unjustified.

This position, however, will not do either. Whether it is wholly unnecessary or not to have recourse to a psycho-analytic story when we have *also* provided a commonsensical one depends on the context and purpose. Consider the boy Jones who is caught doing obscene drawings on the walls of the S.C.R. of a conventional public school. The old housemaster may explain to the new head that the execution of these drawings is a prank, traditionally played on the arrival of a new head, and that Jones was secretly selected to do this by his own fellows. In this context and given the purpose of the two schoolmasters, it is wholly unnecessary for the housemaster to produce anything more than this ordinary commonsensical story. But suppose that the school is a therapeutic community for children who are misfits in ordinary schools. It may then be very necessary for the housemaster to say more – to tell the new head, for example, that Jones was probably quite willing to be selected for this job, since he has an obsessional interest in the obscene, an interest which seems to be tied up with his hatred of his puritanical mother and to which the school prank gave a conventionalized outlet. Similarly with Leonardo. If we are only interested in the traditional history of art, we may not require more than the commonsense, historical story about him. But if we are interested in arriving at a coherent picture of his life as a whole, we may then have to say more. We may then find it necessary to resort to the technicalities of psychoanalysis in order to cover all the data about him, and, in particular, to relate his personality to his paintings and to individually curious items like the kite memory. In doing this we would show how his own personal needs made use of the literary and artistic and other traditions of the time, and through them took the opportunity of conventionalized expression. We would thereby show how cultural circumstances and personal factors of a psycho-analytical kind both contributed to produce an item such as the kite-memory.

The historian's narrative, therefore, does not show that Freud's story is wholly unnecessary and without any justification. What it does do is to reveal that there is not as much point in using Freud's story to cover the items of the kite memory, 'St Anne', and the 'Mona Lisa' as Freud supposed. For in providing an alternative narrative about these items, the historian shows that Freud's story about them is not necessarily compulsory; and that, even if the factors Freud emphasized were at work, their contribution is less than he imagined. It also suggests, moreover, that Leonardo was in general a much less disturbed individual than he appears to be in the picture of him which Freud's essay gives us.

But what is left of this part of Freud's story after the historian of art has finished with it? Does the historian reduce the point of Freud's story *equally* for these three items? Or is there more point left to Freud's interpretation of, say, the 'Mona Lisa' than of the kite memory?

We have good independent evidence that Leonardo became deeply involved in, and obsessed with, the painting of the 'Mona Lisa' and hence that it had a personal significance for him. The historian's story concentrates on the cultural origins of the smile; it does not give a cultural origin to the disturbing character of the face as a whole. This suggests that the historical account of the 'Mona Lisa' does not do much to reduce the point of Freud's story about her, or indeed of any other psychological story about this painting. In contrast, we have no evidence that Leonardo was personally obsessed with the painting of the 'St Anne'; and this picture does not engender the disturbed fascination that the 'Mona Lisa' does. It looks, therefore, as if the historian's story considerably reduces the point of Freud's account of this painting. About the kite memory, we have no independent evidence that this was psychologically important to Leonardo. The only thing that suggests it was important is the fact that Leonardo recorded it, and that it was the only memory he did put on paper. However, the trouble is that the historian's narrative now suggests a psychological explanation of the kite memory quite different from Freud's. It suggests that this memory is a reconstruction of some past experience of the sort Adlerians emphasize – a reconstruction in which he, Leonardo, makes use of a current tradition and which springs from his wishes to be destined for greatness and to become great. So the historian's narrative makes Freud's story about this item look rather insubstantial.

The work of the historian also has a bearing on Freud's remarks about Reitler's article on Leonardo's drawing of coition. We have already discussed the errors that Reitler quite mistakenly claims to have found in this drawing. However, Reitler also points to other errors in it, which he claims are evidence of considerable libidinal repression; and Freud appears to accept this claim. Thus, Reitler points to the poor representation of the female genital, in which the vagina is treated as the *portio uteri* and the lines of the uterus are completely confused; as well as to the misrepresentation of the nipple, which is wrongly given as a single excretory duct, not a number of separate ones.

It is precisely (Reitler says) in the process of portraying the act of procreation that this excessive instinct [of Leonardo] for research has totally failed – obviously only as a result of his even greater sexual repression.

A historian of science may find this contention quite implausible. Thus to O'Malley and Saunders[1] the important thing about this drawing (Q III 3 v.) is that it expresses almost entirely traditional notions on the act of generation, and is an attempt to harmonize the views of Avicenna and Galen. From Galen comes the belief that the sperm is derived from the testes, the 'first cause' of man's existence; from Hippocrates through Avicenna comes the idea that the soul, the 'second cause' of existence, is infused from the spinal cord, the site of the generative faculty. Consequently, the penis has two canals in the drawing – the upper conducting the animal spirit or soul, the latter allowing for passage of sperm and urine. The corrugated appearance of the uterus reflects the medieval idea that its cavity is divided into seven cells. The uterus itself was supposed to expand during coition, as Leonardo shows, and the cervix to open, according to some Arab authors, to embrace the glans penis. On conception it was believed that the blood of the retained menses was carried by the

1. O'Malley, C. D., and Saunders, J. B. de C. M. *Leonardo da Vinci on the Human Body*. New York (Schuman), 1952.

epigastric veins, as illustrated, to the breasts for the formation of milk. On the same sheet as this drawing are longitudinal and transverse sections of the penis, which are quite fanciful in representing the traditional view that it contains two passages. A drawing of the female genitals (Q III, 1 r.), leaves out the labia minora and clitoris; in a later drawing (Q III, 7 r.) the vulva and labia minora are now shown with greater accuracy and detail. In the famous frontal view of the anatomy of the female (Q I, 12 r.), the anatomical details are drawn for the most part from dissections made on animals, in an attempt to represent the Galenical system. The general view that O'Malley and Saunders take is that the reproductive organs of male and female are treated by Leonardo with a curious mixture of fact and fancy. Most of the figures have some objective basis, which is overlaid, however, by traditional theories on function. Again, and this is common in Leonardo's drawings, the earlier figures reflect primitive, medieval theories of generation which later on are replaced by drawings and text in which Galenical ideas predominate. O'Malley and Saunders also reject, in effect, the common belief that Leonardo did a great deal of dissection on human material. On the contrary, it is not certain that he ever became the possessor of a complete cadaver; his remark that he dissected more than ten bodies does not mean that they were complete bodies; and though he was undoubtedly a spectator at others' dissections, his notebooks only give good evidence that he personally dissected about seven distinct human items. These historians conclude that Leonardo was groping in his anatomical studies, as he sought to escape from a debased medieval Aristotelianism through a corrupted Galenism to the independence of science.

Now this historical account leaves the Freud–Reitler

story about the drawing of coition with very little weight. For it is clear that we do not have to appeal to Leonardo's attitude to sex to account for the errors that Reitler pointed out. We can explain these by pointing out that the drawing was primarily a representation of traditional beliefs from which he had not escaped – beliefs that included mistakes about the nature of the uterus, the connexion of the nipples with it, and the behaviour of the uterus and the cervix at copulation. There is nothing surprising about his not doing the dissection of a female cadaver, which would have put him right. He did not do the dissection of a male one either, which would have put him right on the simple matter of the structure of the penis. He did not do any of this partly, no doubt, because he did not have the opportunities, and partly because, like his contemporaries, he had not escaped from a traditional outlook in which fact and fancy were not clearly and carefully distinguished. Hence, as the traditional doctrine stated that the breast milk came via a duct from the uterus, it would not occur normally to Leonardo, or anyone else, to examine cadavers or nursing mothers to find out whether the traditional doctrine was correct or not. So the historical account of this coition figure puts it back into its historical context, and removes its puzzling features in the usual way – by producing a coherent commonsensical narrative about it. The fact that this alternative can be offered reduces the weight of the Freud–Reitler story to negligible proportions.

But in spite of the strength of the criticism from the historians – whether this be directed against Freud's story about the kite memory or his view of the coition figure – Freud's narrative retains certain features which historical criticism does not touch. These features incline us still to cling to it, in whole and in part. Freud's narrative, let us remember, is an attempt to produce a *complete* story about Leonardo, or something approaching one. That is to say, Freud is attempting to cover the whole of Leonardo's life and work, and to fit it together into a coherent picture. Insofar as his story realizes this aim, it has weight and it impresses us. What is more important, the different parts of the whole story, in fitting together, lend one another mutual support. We saw an example of how this worked in our discussion of Leonardo's interest in flight and science. When therefore the historian has done his worst about some one part of Freud's story, such as the kite memory, this part of the story still retains the support that the *rest* of Freud's story gives it; and this fact inclines us to cling to it. Further, Freud's narrative brings Leonardo's life and work into intimate connexion with the inner history of the man, with his private world of unconscious motives, personal experience, and desires. This whole narrative may just be a novel, but it is nevertheless a profoundly interesting and stimulating novel, full of suggestion and insight. In contrast, the narratives of the historians seem flat and superficial. They do not penetrate to the inner recesses of the man; in a way, they tell us nothing about Leonardo – they give us no more understanding of him than we had at the outset. We also cling, therefore, to Freud's narrative because we want the sort of illuminating it offers us. We cling even though we know from the historians that some of this illumination is very probably only apparent and illusory.

7

The historical narratives that we have considered only cover *parts* of Leonardo's life and work. Freud's narrative attempts to provide *complete* coverage of the data, or something approaching this. What reason, or reasons, are there which make it obligatory for us to accept Freud's complete story about Leonardo, rather than some other story of this same sort?

As Freud's narrative has to present a coherent picture of Leonardo, it follows that, if it is not completely coherent, it is not adequate, and hence less obligatory for us than an alternative story which is free from this defect. Is it, then, a coherent story or picture? Unfortunately, this question is only worth asking where the technical theory used to construct a story is a tight and precisely built one. We are then able to determine the logical consequences of any two statements in the story, and so discover definitely whether these two statements are inconsistent. But the technical theory that Freud uses is not of this sort. It is loosely and imprecisely built, so that it is not really worth while asking whether any story constructed by means of it is free from inconsistencies. The same is true of any other, complete narrative that can be offered at the present time. However, if Freud's story is to be a complete narrative of Leonardo's life and work, then it must cover all or most of the facts about him. Insofar as it does not do so – insofar as it leaves out bits and pieces – Freud's story could only claim to be a coherent narrative about *certain aspects* of his life and work. If we then found some alternative story with fewer omissions and a greater coverage than Freud gives us, we should have a reason for accepting this alternative story in preference to Freud's.

Let us ask, therefore: does Freud's story cover all the known facts about Leonardo or does it leave out any items? To this question it is tempting to give an emphatic answer. There are various aspects of Leonardo's life and work that the story does not cover. Thus, it does not deal with his marked personal fastidiousness. It

does not deal with the obvious perfectionism of his art.
Though the story does cover some of the content and
form of his art, it covers very little of it. For example, it
may cover the 'Mona Lisa' and her facial expression.
but it does not include the fact that she sits with folded
hands against a background of rocks. Freud's story may
cover the fact that Leonardo painted the 'St Anne', but
it does not include the fact that the painting takes
pyramidal form, or the particular balance of forms
which it shows. Nor does Freud's story touch on activities such as Leonardo's drawings of animals (which obviously fascinated him from his early years), his drawings and paintings of nature and of plants and flowers,
his essays into architecture and sculpture (for example,
the form of the projected monument to Sforza), the
vitality and ferocity and animal vigour exhibited in his
work for the 'Battle of Anghiari', or the whole theme
and quality of a work like 'St Jerome'. Then, if the
mysterious smile of the later drawings and paintings
conceals a secret of love, as Freud suggests, why the
pointing finger, which appears in some of them? Is this
not also part of the mystery? And did the finger not
first appear very early on in Leonardo's life – in the
Louvre version of The Virgin of the Rocks – when,
according to Freud, Leonardo was still in the full bloom
of creative vigour, and long before the libidinal upsurge
of middle-age, which gave rise, allegedly, to his androgynous figures with Leonardesque smiles? It looks
as if there is an aspect of the Leonardo mystery that
Freud's story simply does not cover. Nor, of course,
does the story cover the obsession of the older Leonardo
with water and cataclysmic destruction; and it passes
over such themes in the notebooks as his pessimism and
his preoccupation with death. In short, and without

going into further details, it is clear that Freud's story is far from providing a complete coverage.

But this tempting and emphatic answer is misleading. The reason is this. If Freud were trying to give us a complete, *scientific* story about Leonardo, *any* failure of coverage would be relevant and worthy of mention. But, as we have already seen, Freud is not trying to do this. He is attempting the less ambitious task of removing the inconsistencies and solving the enigma Leonardo presents. It does not necessarily matter, therefore, if the essay omits to deal with items that a scientific story would have to cover. It only matters if the essay omits to cover items that are concerned with the inconsistencies and enigma that Freud is trying to remove. Thus, it is perfectly true that the essay does not tell us why Leonardo chose to present Mona Lisa with her hands visible (which was a new departure in portrait painting), or why Leonardo was able to represent human flesh as though alive, or why the 'St Anne' embodied the particular balance of forms it does. It is true, too, that the essay does not elucidate the important fact that Leonardo became an artist at all – an omission to which Freud draws attention quite explicitly. But these omissions do not matter because they do not contribute much, if at all, to the enigma that Leonardo exhibits. They do not appear to be inconsistent with anything else we know about him. Moreover, *any* psychological story at present would have great difficulty in covering these items. There is no current story that *can* tell us with any confidence why, for instance, Leonardo chose to paint Mona Lisa with her hands visible. Hence these omissions do not help us to distinguish between the worth of Freud's story and the worth of any other. The only omissions that are relevant are those which contribute to the puzzle Leonardo presents. In Freud's story these seem to centre round various aspects of Leonardo's personality, such as his perfectionism, and round the mystery and strangeness of his art. Consequently, though Freud's narrative has gaps in it, this defect is not nearly as serious as it may seem at first sight.

However, it can be maintained, this defect is quite serious enough. The relevant omissions in Freud's story, it could be said, are important enough to make it unwise of us to rely on this story alone. If we did so, we should only gain a very partial understanding of the character and work of Leonardo. Can we, then, employ these relevant omissions, or gaps, in Freud's narrative to distinguish logically between it and any alternative? Again, unfortunately, it seems doubtful whether we can make much use of them. Certainly we cannot use them with any decisive effect. Suppose we try, and we say to a contemporary analyst: 'Look, Freud's account of Leonardo leaves out this and that and the other relevant thing. Surely these omissions are good objections to his account?' To this challenge the analyst can make quite a good reply. He can reply by using psycho-analytic theory to fill in and make good these omissions in Freud's essay. In other words, he can defend Freud's story by elaborating and developing it to cover the bits and pieces of relevance and importance that Freud does not deal with. Two different circumstances make it possible for a contemporary analyst to do this. Freud's story is an application of psycho-analytic theory; and this theory, like the typical theory in psycho-dynamics and psychopathology is vague and loosely constructed. Accordingly, it is relatively easy to apply and to extend the theory to cover features of Leonardo's personality that were omitted from Freud's early story about him. What is perhaps more important is that Freud produced his story in the early days of psycho-analysis. Since then developments in psycho-analytic theory have taken place which would enable a contemporary analyst to produce a much more sophisticated and better story about Leonardo than Freud did – indeed, a story in which most of the omissions in Freud's own account are made good. When, therefore, we are feeling critical of Freud's essay, it is just as well to remember that his was an early effort, and that better psycho-analytical stories can now be produced.

Still, we are considering Freud's account in this essay, not any later and better version of it. Do the relevant omissions in it help us to decide on its logical weight in comparison with an alternative? The best way of answering this question is to examine an example of a narrative which *is* an alternative to Freud's. Moreover, the ordinary person who reads Freud's essay may not be acquainted with any alternative story at all, or aware of how one can be constructed. In his ignorance he may be fascinated by Freud's essay. He may be trapped into letting the story get a monopolistic hold on him that is logically unwarranted. The simplest way to break this monopoly and to free his imagination is to outline an alternative story to the one Freud has given us.

Let us, then, consider a certain alternative which any contemporary psycho-analyst who is not a dyed-in-the-wool Freudian would perhaps agree was an alternative worth considering. For brevity of reference let us call it the 'A' narrative or story – 'A' being short for 'alternative'. The 'A' narrative, like Freud's, also supposes that certain events occurred in Leonardo's early years which had a great effect upon him. It supposes that in his early years he suffered some great emotional shock or shocks, in which the security he had reposed in some adult or adults was shattered, and his love and affection for them apparently not returned. In other words, it supposes that as a child Leonardo underwent certain experiences which left him bitterly let down, and disastrously hurt and disappointed. These experiences may have centred round Leonardo's removal from Caterina to his father's house, which to him may have been an emotional betrayal and an injustice both by Caterina and his father. But it is not necessary for the 'A' story to say, or seriously speculate about, what these traumatic events may have been. Next, the story also supposes that during and after these shattering events, the personal relations inside the family groups concerned were such that the child's deep disappointment was not repaired. For example, the personal relations may have been of a warm-hearted and conscientious, but utterly superficial and unseeing kind, in which the adults failed to make genuine contact with the child. Or, as an only child in a household of adults, his own childish needs may have been swamped and forgotten in an atmosphere that used his own intelligence and precocity to treat him as a little adult, with the consequence that he never had the opportunity as a child to learn how to love adults or children. The family relations, therefore, whatever they may have been, served to entrench or fixate Leonardo's fears of the dangers of expressing himself emotionally at all. Emotionally bitten once or a few times, he became forever shy. Hence his inability as an adult to reveal himself emotionally and develop an affectionate relationship with anyone. Hence his great reserve, his impenetrability, and the personal mystery that he presented to his contemporaries as well as to us. It is not surprising, therefore, that he should write as follows in the *Treatise on Painting*:

In truth great love springs from great knowledge of the beloved object, and if you know it but little you will be able to love it only a little or not at all. . . .

Given his distrust of his own feelings, he will have to keep them constantly in check, and one way of doing so is to be distrustful, suspicious, and sceptical of all those he finds arousing his feelings; to ask himself whether he knows these people well enough to justify or warrant him giving them his love, or whether they will not let him down also, as he was let down in the past.

At adolescence Leonardo is faced by fresh problems. With the development of the adult sexual impulse, he is threatened by the danger of personal and emotional involvement. He deals with this in two ways. First, he completes the development of the severe conscience that he brings from childhood. This severe and puritanical conscience is revealed right through his notebooks – for example, in his repudiation of the struggle for money, and his hatred of cruelty; in the sublime and austere character of the whole; in his total rejection of sexuality. 'Whoso curbs not lustful desires,' he writes, 'puts himself on a level with the beasts. You can have neither a greater nor a less dominion than that over yourself. It is easier to resist at the beginning than at the end' (H 119 (24 v.) r.). Leonardo also dealt with the problem of his adolescence by absorbing his sexual energies into his creative work as an artist, craftsman, and scientific inquirer. As he said himself: 'Intellectual passion drives out sensuality' (C.A. 358 v.a.). The upshot was to make himself impotent. From his early disappointments he developed into a sexually negative individual, a man whose genital functioning was inhibited.

But the aspects of himself that he has denied – the aspects to which he has failed to do justice – persist in breaking through and coming to the surface. Because he has repudiated the affective side of his life, his repudiation contributes to make him obsessionally concerned with it. But as his obsessional interest cannot be directly expressed, it comes out in displaced and substitute forms. It comes out in the emotionally intense products of his art. It comes out in his obsessional attempt to grasp and exhibit perfectly the beauty and truth of nature. But just as he cannot ever achieve what he really needs – namely, love and inner peace – so this goal of truth and beauty must be placed beyond the limits of his own powers. Consequently, he always places his standards of perfection beyond his own actual achievements and powers. Hence his perfectionism – his search for what is to him unattainable. Given this personal compulsion, he is obviously disposed to adopt an epistemological position that does something to make his search for the unattainable a rational and justifiable enterprise; and indeed it looks as if he did actually come to hold a view of this sort. For in his *Treatise on Painting* he contends with passion that painting is a scientific activity, and it is the business of the painter and artist to present correctly, and therefore perfectly, the truth about nature. But clearly it is logically impossible *not* to abstract from certain features of nature when one paints it. Therefore, his epistemological position sets Leonardo a logically unobtainable goal. It is not possible to present on a piece of paper the whole truth about an item in nature. In this way his articulate attitude about his work – which his obsessional search for the perfect disposes him to adopt – serves in turn to reinforce his obsession.

Given, however, that this is the aim or goal of his work, it follows that he will be frustrated in his attempt to realize it. Therefore his interest in something – his impulse to understand it scientifically and to represent the truth about it visually – will exhaust itself before he has finished with it. He will then move on to something else, in search of fresh stimulus. Hence, in part, the catalogue of unfinished works. He dispersed his energies over a large range of fields, because he was a man of exceptional and many-sided abilities, whose interest could be aroused by almost any problem; and because he lived in an age which still accepted the medieval view that a complete knowledge of nature and spirit was attainable and could be embraced by one man. His gradual transition from art to science was not, as Freud would have us believe, a regression, but the understandable outcome of his obsessional attempts to reach an unattainable goal. When he tries to paint nature in the way he sets himself, he is inevitably frustrated and disappointed. But he is not in a personal position to face up to this fact. So, in effect, he gives up painting and art, and moves over to scientific inquiry. In this way he saves himself from the frustrating disappointment of, to him, unsatisfactory work in art, and yet he preserves his whole orientation, conscious and unconscious, to himself and his work. For in scientific inquiry he can now concentrate on discovering what, in his view, he needs to know about men and things before he is in a position to communicate this knowledge pictorially. In this way he can give scope to his obsessional search for perfection, while avoiding the inevitable pains of trying realistically to end the search in any one product of his genius.

But about 1500 Leonardo came to face the typical crisis of middle-age. Other submerged and denied aspects of his nature began to stir about this time – namely, his need to love and be loved, his need for genuine human affection and sexual satisfaction. When he came to paint Mona Lisa, he was aroused by her; she threatened to bring the submerged aspects of himself to the surface. Leonardo dealt with this danger by using her to symbolize the several-sided character of his difficulties. To him she became an object of loving approach and of frightened avoidance. She was the mother who had loved and nurtured him, and who, having completed her mothering task to her own self-satisfaction, had discarded him. She was the woman who held out the promise of adult love and sexual satisfaction, and yet who dwelt beyond the bounds of the attainable. She was the person who offered him the quiet authority and security of inner peace, and also the threat that he would lose his independence and personal isolation – the menace that she would devour him in the process of loving him and giving him peace. She was the figure who offered him the hope of real intimacy with another soul; and the fear that he would not succeed in realizing this hope of achieving genuine intimacy – the fear that, in spite of his efforts she would remain a being apart, remote, mysterious, and impenetrable. In painting Mona Lisa he put into the picture the different facets of his own personal conflict that she as the model brought to the surface. Leonardo did this in a way that makes the painting the perfect ambiguous figure. This is why it is so remarkable. It arouses in us subtle and endless contrasts of ambivalence about Woman. In this painting Leonardo has created an archetypal image of an *anima* figure – to employ Jung's terms. Hence its fascination for us.

However, to Leonardo the painting also represented a partial resolution of his crisis. In putting into it the different facets of his own conflict, he achieved an expression of the conflict, and a measure of detachment from and mastery over it. So the painting of the Mona Lisa helped him to achieve some inner harmony, rather in the way that the patients of Jungians appear to do when they come to produce and articulate mandala-like figures. After this crisis Leonardo went on to express and master his difficulties in a similar manner. In particular, his paintings retained the central feature of the ambiguous Mona Lisa – namely the smile. But the solution he achieved in this way was far from complete. For among the aspects of his personality that he had denied was the craving for sexual experience and union. When this started coming up, he could not master it by means of the Mona Lisa figures and their features – the aid these could give him was not sufficient. He went on therefore to try to deal with this side of his problem by producing the androgynous figures of his later years – works in which male and female were blissfully united.

As we have seen, his obsessional search for the perfection of truth and beauty was bound to be disappointing, intellectually and personally. The chief source of his intellectual dissatisfaction is that, even if he were to communicate the truth and the beauty of nature and of man perfectly, he would not and could not communicate the secret of existence, namely, why God, Nature, and Life are here at all – the ultimate mystery of Being. When his dissatisfaction about this comes to the surface, he expresses and tries to master it in his usual way. He exhibits the mystery of Being in his work. His figures become quite unfathomable, very mysterious and occult; and the finger points to something outside the painting and beyond the limits of our world, to something that neither he nor we can say or solve. The chief source of his personal disappointment lies in the fact that his obsessional search for perfection is a symptom of his own personal tragedy. This search, being a displacement, did not bring him the satisfaction he sought by means of it. So, as old age came on, his unhappiness, his sense of personal failure, came to the surface. He came unconsciously to despair of ever achieving inner peace. Largely because of the way in which the security and happiness of his early years was shattered, he had developed a strong, unconscious dislike of the human race in general – a misanthropy that is revealed in many places in his notebooks. In old age he now lets loose his resentment and his hatred of man. He wishes to die and to destroy the world. This is what is revealed in his drawings of cataclysmic destruction. Here he invokes what he believes to be the most powerful force in nature, namely water. He invokes it to destroy mankind and all its works, and to drown himself and his own despair in the flood of universal chaos.

This, then, is an outline of narrative 'A' – an alternative to the one Freud has given us. Clearly, it has affinities with Freud's and it is definitely post-Freudian in nature. But it is not orthodox Freudian psycho-analysis. It is more akin to the sort of narrative that a person influenced by Jung's thought or eclectic psychodynamics would provide. It also, perhaps, presents the sort of psychological picture of Leonardo that is implicit in the work of a scholar such as Heydenreich.[1] By outlining this alternative, we may do something to free the ordinary reader from the fascinated hold that Freud's account may have upon him. But how does this alternative help us to decide on the adequacy of Freud's narrative?

It will be evident to anyone who has listened to clinical discussions on ward rounds, in case conferences, and similar places, that there is a close resemblance between the discussion among psychiatrists, and others,

1. Heydenreich, Ludwig H. *Leonardo da Vinci*. London (Allen & Unwin), 1954.

over a difficult mental case, and a discussion over the pros and cons of Freud's story about Leonardo and the 'A' alternative we outlined. What a psychiatrist does is to try to bring the case in question within the framework of some theoretical scheme or set of concepts and generalizations, or, conversely, to fit the latter to the particular case. Different psychiatrists are apt each to have his own preferred and slightly different scheme or set of concepts. In attempting to fit a particular scheme to the case, what happens typically is that certain features of the case turn out quite easy to fit into the the scheme, whereas others prove more difficult; and that the scheme throws up certain illuminating suggestions about the case which may be worth following up, whereas it underplays and even neglects other features that alternative schemes will point to or emphasize. Which particular story about a case a psychiatrist, or other discussant, chooses at a case conference will depend primarily on his theoretical predilections; and in the absence of further new information about the case, rational discussion can only be continued by going on to examine these theoretical predilections themselves.

Similarly with the discussion about Leonardo. Here Freud and a discussant are trying each to fit his own theoretical scheme on to the data of Leonardo. It is clear that each scheme – Freud's and alternative 'A' – fits some aspects of Leonardo with ease, omits some and has more difficulties with others, and that each sheds its own limited amount of light. Thus, it is clear that the concepts we use to construct the 'A' story are able to deal easily with Leonardo's personal relations and his great reserve, his obsessionalism and perfectionism in art and science, and the misanthropy and despair of his old age. This alternative – at least when fully elaborated – would obviously give a student of Leonardo a great deal of illumination on these aspects of his personality. On the other hand, the concepts used in 'A' give us only a thin story about Leonardo's psychological make-up (or 'inner dynamics'); and about his erotic and sexual life. In these regions of his personality the 'A' scheme is relatively unexciting and unilluminating. In contrast, Freud's theoretical scheme deals more easily with Leonardo's inner dynamics, his erotic and sexual life and the details of his inner development. Freud may be quite wrong in saying that Leonardo was a homosexual, that later he regressed first from art into science, and then – with 'Mona Lisa' – into an art that was a manifestation of his pre-Oedipal stage of development. But what Freud offers us here, though wrong possibly, is detailed and penetratingly suggestive. In any case, it may be easier to cover personal items, such as his fastidiousness, by a development of Freud's story rather than by the 'A' alternative, or a development of it.

What Freud has difficulty in dealing with are Leonardo's intellectual and aesthetic interests, the range and the variety of his work, his perfectionism, and the development of his middle and old age. One feels tempted to say that what Freud tells us on these topics is thin and insufficient. On the other hand, Freud uses his concepts to cover the specific item of the kite memory. When we constructed alternative 'A', we did not use its concepts to cover this item. By including the kite memory within his narrative, Freud ensures that it both gains and loses in strength. It gains in strength just because it shows that, unlike the 'A' story, it can cover a highly specific and singular item such as this memory. It loses because in covering this item Freud is applying his scheme in a way that produces a result which lacks

logical weight, and raises doubts about the validity
of this application. It is important to emphasize this
weakness in Freud's story just because he places so
much importance on his interpretation of the kite
memory. Of course, we *could* have developed the 'A'
story to cover the kite memory – by, for example, using
the semi-Adlerian interpretation of it we have suggested
before. But there is much to be said for not attempting
this. The 'A' story may be all the stronger just because
it does not speculate about this specific item of the kite
memory, thereby saving us from the trap that en-
snared Freud – the trap of attaching undue importance
and weight to the interpretation of this single item.
Then, again, alternative 'A' has the advantage of being
a much *simpler* story than Freud's. It accounts for the
central mystery of Leonardo and the puzzling character
of his art without resorting to complicated hypotheses
about erotic fixation on his mother, repressed sexual
curiosity, regression to the oral stage, and the like.
Furthermore, alternative 'A' is much more commonsensical than Freud's story, and initially much more
plausible in consequence. To this, naturally, a Freudian
can reply that the simplicity of a narrative is not a
necessary condition for its truth. The 'A' story is only
simple and close to commonsense because it is so superficial. It omits and underplays aspects of Leonardo's
life which have to be understood and which Freud does
attempt to penetrate.

When we have worked through the points of strength
and weakness in both narratives – where they fit easily
and awkwardly, what they can cover easily and what
they omit or under-emphasize, where they are suggestive and illuminating and where they are not – there is
nothing more we can do. It is evident that the particular
story one is inclined to choose about Leonardo will

depend on which conceptual scheme, or theory, one prefers. If one's preference is for a classical Freudian scheme, one will opt for Freud's story, or some contemporary elaboration of it. One will then regard as relatively unimportant or insignificant those features of Leonardo's life and work that the Freudian story omits, underplays, finds it difficult to cover, and is not illuminating about. On the other hand, if one prefers a more Jungian scheme, one may opt for the alternative 'A' which we outlined, or some variant of it; and again, one will regard the omissions, and so forth, of this story as relatively unimportant. At this point, any further discussion about Freud's essay will have to move on to discuss other things. The two outstanding questions we may then find ourselves discussing are these. (1) What reasons are there for and against these different theoretical preferences? That is to say, what are the merits of the rival schemes or theories? (2) Quite apart from the relative merits of Freud's scheme, how legitimate is it to apply this scheme – derived chiefly as it is from the psycho-analysis of living people and patients – to a dead-and-gone historical figure?

8

Let us take up the question of legitimacy first. In applying his theory to Leonardo, Freud relies on an argument from analogy. Consider again the kite memory. Freud's account of it can be exhibited in the following schema:

Patients who report memories of the kite sort are apt to have homosexual wishes.

Leonardo reports a kite memory.

Therefore we have good ground for believing that Leonardo has homosexual wishes.

Likewise with the data as a whole which we have about Leonardo. He tries to apply to this the story he would apply if Leonardo were a patient. The application can be expressed in this schema:

A patient who exhibits such and such a pattern of data is likely to be a person with a psychological make-up and pathology of this sort, namely . . .

Leonardo exhibits such and such a pattern of data.

Therefore we have good reason to believe that he has a make-up and pathology of this same sort, namely . . .

How strong is this argument? Let us ignore the difference in logical form between it and comparable arguments in natural science, and therefore pass by the technical difficulties about it that will exercise the logician and the philosopher. The historian of art is likely to say at once that the argument is weak because the analogy is a poor one. It may be the case, for example, that patients who report memories of the kite sort are apt to have homosexual wishes. But there is an important difference between present-day patients and Leonardo, the difference, namely, that the latter, unlike most of the former, was acquainted with similar legends and pictures about kites and birds, as we have already noted. Hence the mere fact that Leonardo reported a kite memory does not make him resemble present-day patients in the other relevant respects. Freud is not entitled, therefore, to argue that we have *good* ground for believing that Leonardo has homosexual wishes. At most he could conclude that we have *a* ground for believing this.

There is another weakness in the argument which disturbs psychoanalysts, psychiatrists, and others in this field. It is doubtful whether Freud's narrative about the kite memory, or about Leonardo as a whole, can satisfy any of the criteria which analysts and others do in practice use to assess the worth of a psycho-analytical narrative about a patient, or about some item in his life. If this doubt is justified, Freud's argument by analogy here differs from the way it is used in the ordinary or standard psycho-analytic context. The consequence of this is to make the whole application of psycho-analytic theory to Leonardo a much more tentative and risky business than the bare bones of the argument from analogy may lead us to suppose.

We can exhibit the nature of this doubt in the following way. Let us imagine that Leonardo was actually a patient of a contemporary analyst, and that he had just produced the kite memory in the course of analysis. Suppose that the analyst at once interpreted this to himself and to us as the manifestation of homosexual wishes, in the way Freud has described. Let us imagine that we challenged him to support this interpretative story. He could defend it as follows. He could say that, if it is true, certain other things will also be true of Leonardo.

(1) A homosexual trend will be revealed in many different types of material in the course of Leonardo's analysis.

(2) The unconscious homosexual trend so revealed will fit together coherently, and so ring true.

(3) This interpretation of the kite memory will be consistent with what is already known in the course of analysis about Leonardo.

(4) This interpretation, when used appropriately by the analyst, will assist the further development of the analysis. It will turn out to be helpful and not obstructive.

These four items are, in effect, four criteria that analysts use in practice to assess the weight of an interpretation. In other words, our analyst could defend his interpretation of the kite memory by saying that the whole and subsequent course of Leonardo's analysis will show whether the interpretation satisfies these four criteria or not. In so far as they are progressively satisfied, we will have better and better reason to accept this interpretation as correct. In so far as they are not progressively satisfied, we will have better and better reason to regard it as mistaken.

Obviously it is very doubtful whether these criteria are applicable to Freud's interpretation of the kite memory. Numbers 3 and 4 are definitely ruled out, because Leonardo is not with us to be analysed. However, it could be argued that, though numbers 1 and 2 are not applicable as they stand, analogues of 1 and 2 may be so. Thus, if we loosen criteria 1 and 2 to allow us to cover the rest of the data about Leonardo which the historical record reveals, we could then ask whether these two analogous criteria are applicable to Freud's interpretation of the kite memory. For we could ask whether a homosexual trend is revealed in the many different types of material contained in the full historical record; and we could also ask whether the unconscious homosexual trend so revealed fits together coherently, and hence rings true. But it is clear that, in this loosened form, these two criteria are rather weak; they serve merely to point to features of Freud's story about the kite memory which are logically inconclusive. Thus, if we try to show that the story satisfies the loosened criterion 1, all we can succeed in doing is to show that it gains support from the fact that other features of Leonardo's record lend themselves to a similar, homosexual type of interpretation. This is far from conclusive, because, as we have seen, the data of Leonardo are open, severally and jointly, to quite a different, non-homosexual type of interpretation. If we try to show that Freud's story about the kite satisfies the loosened criterion 2, all we can succeed in doing is to show that it helps to produce a coherent narrative about the data as a whole that Leonardo gives us. But the *same* claim could, and would undoubtedly, be made for a different interpretation of the kite memory, which formed part of an *alternative* story about Leonardo. Therefore criterion 2 in its loosened form also fails to differentiate logically between Freud's kite interpretation and an alternative.

It is clear that the same sort of conclusion is true of Freud's narrative as a whole. When an analyst deals with a patient, he usually works with and is guided by a tentative, developing, and perhaps not even expressly formulated narrative about the patient's psychological make-up and pathology. If we challenge him over this story, he can support it by means of criteria analogous to the four just considered. But Freud cannot support his narrative about Leonardo as a whole in this way; for it is evident that these analogous criteria are either not applicable to the narrative at all, or are only applicable to it in a weak and inconclusive way. When an analyst, or psychiatrist, or psychotherapist is faced by an actual case which he finds difficult to understand, he and his colleagues may form tentative but alternative stories about the patient. In these circumstances, a story serves to produce all sorts of expectations about the patient; and the alternative stories which are canvassed are apt to produce *different* expectations. Now the living patient in analysis is constantly producing fresh material, and this fresh material may serve to realize some of these expectations about him and not others. The analyst will look to this new material to help him to distinguish between the alternative stories, and so decide which one is to be preferred. But Freud cannot make use of fresh data from analytic sessions to distinguish between his story about Leonardo and an alternative. Indeed, with one exception, neither he nor we can make use of any fresh data at all about Leonardo, as the data are fixed in the historical record. It is quite clear, therefore, that there is this very important logical difference between a narrative about a living patient and Freud's story about Leonardo.

The one exception just referred to is the new material that may be uncovered by further historical research. In order for this to be helpful, the data in the material must be relevant; and the more relevant the more helpful. But the new historical data that may be uncovered in the future are likely to resemble the usual sort of historical material we already have about Leonardo. Now this material – the known facts about him, the notebooks, the paintings, and so on – is very massive and suggestive; but it is not very close to the sort of material that an analyst, psychiatrist, or clinical psychologist would ideally prefer to have about him. What these workers would prefer to have is material sufficiently close to the alternative narratives we can spin about Leonardo to enable them to decide with assurance which narrative is the strongest. But the historical material does not provide the sort of data that a clinical worker would try to obtain from Leonardo – if he were with us – in an attempt to investigate, say, Freud's suggestion that he was a homosexual. It seems unlikely that any fresh historical material will be different in this respect from the old. Hence it is unlikely that any new data will help us to settle the strength of Freud's narrative, in the typical way that fresh material about a patient helps us in analogous circumstances.

The conclusion, then, is that Freud's narrative about

the kite memory or about Leonardo as a whole cannot satisfy two of the four criteria analysts apply to their narratives about patients, and only satisfies the remaining two in a form so weak as to make them of little help to us. This means that Freud's application of psychoanalytic theory to Leonardo in this essay cannot be confirmed or disconfirmed in the way that is characteristic of psycho-analytic stories about patients. Consequently, though Freud's essay is based on an argument from analogy of the sort that is typical of psychoanalytic discourse, the essay is a much more tentative and uncertain enterprise than the standard narrative about a patient. All this makes it clear that Freud's essay is not a typical, and therefore good, example of the sort of narrative he usually uses and offers about a patient.

How legitimate, then, is Freud's attempt to apply psycho-analytic theory to Leonardo? How far was he justified in writing this essay? It is tempting to say that Freud was quite justified in giving us his essay, because it is a *jeu d'esprit* which has raised questions of great importance about Leonardo, and which has forced us to look at artists in quite new and exciting ways. No doubt, if we do treat it as a *jeu d'esprit*, we cannot object to it. It becomes a justifiable exercise in intellectual high spirits that has had a great effect. But it is very doubtful if Freud himself, or the orthodox analytic tradition, has regarded the essay in this light. To Freud the essay was an undertaking that 'did not perhaps provide any certain results' (Chapter Six), but clearly it was not just a piece of fun to him. Ernest Jones tells us in his biography that it was one of Freud's favourite works, and refers to one of Freud's letters in which he says that he, Freud, was unmoved by the 'horror' people had expressed about it, because he was so pleased with it himself.[1] Ernest Jones himself takes the essay quite seriously; and it has recently been described as a 'classic of psycho-analysis.'[2] So perhaps it is safer to regard the essay as something stronger than a mere *jeu d'esprit*.

But how much stronger? Some analysts may be tempted to swing to the opposite extreme, and to regard the essay as a diagnostic and psychopathological narrative which has to be treated in exactly the same sort of way as a standard application of psycho-analysis to an individual patient. But we have seen that this essay is very different from the standard psycho-analytic narrative about a patient. Hence, if we view the essay in this light, it becomes an illegitimate application of psycho-analytic theory. On this view, Freud is trying to do with Leonardo what cannot be done, and should not be attempted.

A more cautious analyst, however, may be inclined to take up a more moderate position – which he could explain in the following way. Consider a patient who enters a mental hospital. He is examined and a full psychiatric report drafted about him. This report will include a diagnosis and, where it is deemed relevant, an account of his psychopathology. But if the patient is a difficult case to understand, the report may be very tentative about diagnosis and psychopathology; it may even not include either; or it may include *more* than one story about diagnosis and psychopathology. Suppose that, at the case conference on this puzzling case, an analyst is invited to contribute; and suppose that he

1. Jones, Ernest. *Sigmund Freud Life and Work*, Vol. Two. London (The Hogarth Press), 1955.
2. Wohl, R. R., and Trosman, H. 'A Retrospect of Freud's *Leonardo*, An Assessment of a Psychoanalytic Classic.' *Psychiatry*, 18, 27–39. 1955.

spins a psycho-analytic story about the patient. Here the data or material of the case are temporarily fixed or given in the psychiatric report that has been presented to the conference. They are fixed for the time being in this historical record. In these circumstances, the analyst is likely to put forward his story tentatively. He will intend it to be taken seriously, and yet he will admit that he is speculating. He thinks that his story, or something like it, may be true; but he recognizes that it is only one among other alternatives. He concedes implicitly that it may be off the mark; and yet he hopes that it will not be, and that it will turn out to be a fruitful suggestion. In applying his theory to the difficult case in this way, the analyst is doing something that is not only legitimate, but very appropriate and often helpful. Now the moderate analyst can say that *this* is the way in which Freud is applying his theory to Leonardo. What Freud is doing is something very akin to what the analyst did at the case conference. He is offering a speculative story that is meant to be taken seriously.

It is clear that, if we describe Freud's essay in this cautious way, what he did becomes a perfectly legitimate enterprise. But, though we can legitimize the essay in this way, we can only do so at a price. The price is that analysts give up regarding it as the *only* story, or the only *sort* of story, that is or can be correct. They have to recognize that other alternatives can be produced that deserve consideration. Though these may all be post-Freudian alternatives, and in this sense also psycho-analytic in character, they are not alternatives of the sort that Freud himself would have accepted. What therefore analysts will have to give up is Freud's own way of regarding or thinking about his essay. They will have to say that Freud is at fault in supposing that it necessarily provides the only entreé to the truth about Leonardo.

9

The argument from analogy on which Freud's essay is based moves us for an additional reason which we have not mentioned yet. Consider again the schema of the argument about the data as a whole:

A patient who exhibits such and such a pattern of data is likely to be a person with a psychological make-up and pathology of this sort, namely . . .

Leonardo exhibits such and such a pattern of data.

Therefore we have good reason to believe that he has a make-up and pathology of this same sort, namely . . .

The strength or weight of this argument depends, in part, on the strength of the major premiss. But the latter is part of the whole classical theory of psycho-analysis which Freud has applied to Leonardo. The strength of the major premiss, therefore, also depends on the weight of the theory to which it belongs. Now the weight of psycho-analytic theory is the additional reason that moves us to accept the argument from analogy. The more weight we are inclined to attach to the theory, the more will we be moved to accept the argument and therefore the essay. What weight, then, should we attach to the classical theory Freud used? As different psychiatrists, analysts, and others, are apt to attach different weights to different theories, and to have different theoretical preferences, what reasons are there for choosing to use classical analysis to understand Leonardo rather than some other theory? Is it more weighty than the others? What, in short, are the merits of the rival theories in this field?

These are very large technical questions which have

been much discussed in recent years, but to which no generally accepted answer can yet be given. Accordingly, we shall not attempt to answer them here. We shall merely consider *one* reason for this inconclusive state of affairs – a reason which also throws some further light on the nature of Freud's essay.

The psycho-analytic theory Freud used, like psycho-analytic theory in general, is based chiefly on the evidence obtained from the analysis of patients. This analysis is carried out by means of what we shall call, for brevity, psycho-analytic method. This method has been quite extensively used, in different forms, over the last fifty years or so. But it has not been subjected to a careful scientific investigation in order to determine its validity. It is quite uncertain, therefore, how valid the method is. So naturally the theories that are based on its use are equally uncertain in evidential and scientific status. We can bring out some of the uncertainties about psycho-analytic method by considering the use Freud puts it to in order to explain Leonardo's kite memory.

The kernel of Freud's explanation of this memory is that in it Leonardo reveals to us that he has an unconscious concern with the homosexual idea of an act of fellatio. Freud supports this, as we have seen, by the usual argument from analogy.

Patients who produce under analysis a memory of this kite type are typically patients with this unconscious homosexual concern.
Leonardo has produced a kite type of memory.
Hence he too has this unconscious homosexual concern.

Suppose we now challenge an analyst to produce the evidence to support the major premiss of this argument, namely that patients under analysis who produce a kite-type memory typically have this unconscious homo-sexual concern. In other words, we ask what is the analyst's evidence for holding that the tail of a kite (or something similar) represents a penis for a patient, and that beating a tail against and within his lips in his cradle (or something similar) represents the insertion and sucking of a penis? To this challenge the analyst could reply: 'A memory-report of this sort by a patient is what we call a phantasy. That is, roughly, it is the report of something that did not occur, but which is the transformation of some past experience in accordance with an unconscious wish of the patient. Reports of the kite type are transformations of past experiences at the breast, and reveal an unconscious wish to suck a penis.'

But suppose we challenge the analyst again. What is the evidence that the kite type of report is a transform-ation of some past experience, that the particular experience is one of sucking at the breast, and that the unconscious concern is to suck a penis? To this chal-lenge the analyst might be tempted to offer the usual or typical reply. 'The supporting evidence', he might say, 'is to be found in the following facts. When in the course of the analysis of a patient, we analysts interpret the kite type of report, and related material, in this way, we find that these interpretations are apt to satisfy the four criteria we have already outlined and discussed; and the patient comes, after a time, to recognize for himself that these interpretations are true, including the hypothesis that he has an unconscious concern with sucking a penis.'

Unfortunately, this typical reply from the analyst is far from being conclusive. The chief difficulty about it seems to be this. If the procedure of psycho-analysis were *only* one of discovery, if it simply *revealed the facts* about a patient to us and to himself, then this usual defence by the analyst might be adequate. But there is good reason to believe that the procedure of psycho-analysis is not one of straightforward discovery and revelation, like the standard methods of science. There is good reason to believe that it is a procedure which, whatever else it does, also *transforms* the patient in the direction indicated by the sort of interpretations the analyst uses about him; and that, in doing this, it helps to make the interpretations used about the patient appear to be true of him. The way this happens – though very complex and not yet adequately explored – can be grasped in outline when we take note of two features of psycho-analytic method.

(*a*) The procedure of psycho-analysis is tension-rousing in a way which, during the initial period, disorganizes the patient's beliefs about himself, attitudes in general, and so forth; and therefore makes him labile and hence suggestible.

(*b*) The analyst is concerned, *inter alia*, to understand the mass of material the patient is offering him. He tries to do this by ordering the material in terms of the concepts and generalizations of the particular brand of psycho-analytic theory he prefers. In so doing, he is constantly *seeing in* the material all sorts of subtle cues, fleeting items, nuances of attitudes and conduct, etc., which an analyst from a different tradition and using a different brand of theory might not see in the patient's material. In the light of what the analyst sees in the material, as well as of his own judgement, and so forth, he offers his interpretations to the patient.

Now, in these special circumstances of analysis, these two features, (*a*) and (*b*), have a profound effect. The suggestible patient comes to accept the interpretations offered him and to transform himself in the direction they indicate. These interpretations will then satisfy the four criteria discussed, but this fact is not sufficient to show that they are true. It is only sufficient to show that the analyst and patient are being jointly successful in changing the patient's personality and outlook. The fact that the patient comes to accept the truth of these interpretations is only enough to show that he has been converted to the new point of view about himself, not that they are true of him. But, as the interpretations helped to transform him in a certain direction, they helped to change him into a person of whom these interpretative remarks seem to be correct or true. We are all familiar with the well-known objection to psycho-analysis that Freudian analysts tend to have Freudian patients, Jungian analysts Jungian patients, and so on. The explanation of this and related facts may lie, in part, in the two features of analytic method we have just emphasized, and in the profound effect they exert in analysis.

Now let us return to Freud's interpretation of the kite memory, and the challenge to produce evidence in support of it. It is clear why the typical reply from the analyst is far from conclusive. He is challenged to produce the evidence in support of the generalization that 'patients who produce under analysis the kite type of memory typically have the unconscious homosexual concern Freud described'. It is not sufficient to reply by saying that in the course of analysis analysts discover that, when they interpret a kite-type memory, and related material, they find the homosexual interpretation of this item satisfies the criteria mentioned, and is accepted by the patient. In other words, it is not sufficient to say that this interpretation helps along the course of the analysis, helps them to spin a coherent psycho-analytical story about the patient and so understand him better, and so forth. It is not sufficient to reply in this vein because the very procedure of analysis itself may contribute to make the homosexual interpretation of the kite memory help along the course of the analysis, make it acceptable to the patient and so apparently true of him. The clinical evidence of psychoanalysis, therefore, does not provide conclusive support for the generalization that patients under analysis who produce a kite type of memory typically have an unconscious homosexual concern. But this generalization is the major premiss of the argument from analogy which Freud uses to support his account of Leonardo's kite memory. It follows that the clinical evidence from psycho-analysis in support of this major premiss is not conclusive, and hence that the whole argument is weaker than analysts normally suppose. Indeed, the position is even worse than this. If the outcome of psycho-analytic method on a patient is even only *in part* the artefact of the method itself, it follows that, unless we know *what* part is not genuine, any generalizations based on the use of psycho-analytic method will be infected with uncertainty. We shall not know what weight to attach to them. At its worst, therefore, it may be that when Freud spins us a story about Leonardo wishing to suck a penis, he, Freud, is himself just the victim or the prisoner of his own method. He may have been trapped by it into a set of beliefs about personality and its development which are delusive, in part or possibly even in whole. In giving us his interpretations of Leonardo's memory, Freud may merely be revealing to us his own delusions about mankind.

The ordinary reader of Freud's essay will probably not be acquainted with the details of psycho-analytic procedure, and of the sort of thing that happens in analysis. Consequently he may be unable to pass any judgement for himself on its validity. However, the essay itself is valuable here, since it throws some light on the sort of thing that goes on. Thus, we have drawn attention to the fact that in analysis the analyst is constantly *seeing things in* the material in the attempt to order and understand it. It is evident to us all, not merely to the psychologist, that this is a hazardous business. For the analyst will see in the material the sort of thing he is on the look-out for. He will read into the material features that an analyst of a different brand will not see there, and that the ordinary person will not see either; and the analyst will go on to use what he sees in the material as the kernel of an interpretation. Now, for reasons connected with the artefact-producing character of analysis, it is difficult usually to pin down examples where the analyst has read things into the material which are just not there, and where, accordingly, the interpretation he offers is just false. But in this essay Freud gives us one excellent example of this very thing, and another example of something close to it.

We have noted that Freud was misled by the German translation he used into supposing that the bird in the kite memory was a vulture. The first example is the 'remarkable discovery' that Freud agreed had been made about the 'St Anne' by the analyst Oskar Pfister, 'even if', Freud acknowledged, 'one may not feel inclined to accept it without reserve'. Pfister claimed to have discovered the outline of a vulture in the drapery of Mary, and pointed out that the right-hand end of the spread-out tail leads to the mouth of the child. It is clear that, as Freud's whole reference to a vulture is a mistake, it is highly probable that Leonardo did not unconsciously conceal a vulture in the picture at all. Yet a vulture is just what Pfister saw in it; and Freud was sufficiently impressed to call this 'a remarkable discovery'. In short, Pfister and Freud saw things in the picture which very probably are just not there, and any interpretation that assumes Leonardo had unconsciously concealed a vulture in the picture is almost certainly false. The second example is Freud's interpretation of the vulture phantasy. If Freud is to give a homosexual interpretation of this which is *complete*, one of the things he has to do is to explain how Leonardo comes to substitute a vulture for his mother. This Freud proceeds to do. He gives us a story the central point of which is that Leonardo was supposed to be acquainted with an ancient fable in which all vultures are females, and which he used unconsciously to produce his phantasy. Now Leonardo may not have had a knowledge of this fable, but Freud is prepared to see in the historical record sufficient evidence to show that he was acquainted with it. Let us presume that Freud is right here, and that Leonardo had a knowledge of it. Freud is also prepared to read into the situation a psychological connexion between this knowledge and the apparent fact of the vulture phantasy. But we know that there was no such connexion whatever, because we know that the phantasy was not in fact about vultures at all. So Freud's story is a piece of speculation which is unnecessary and false. The interpretation he offers us here is just incorrect. We can tell that this is the case in this instance, because we are fortunately placed in having an independent knowledge of the facts. But how can we be sure that *other* parts of Freud's story about Leonardo are not also the outcome of reading Freudian things into Leonardo's life and work, and also, therefore, pieces of speculation which are false? The parts of Freud's essay where he is concerned with the phantasy of the vulture are valuable and instructive to us just because they are wrong. In being wrong, they exhibit clearly and briefly one of the central difficulties about the validity of psycho-analytic method.

We have noted that at the present time there are rival theories or schemes in the field, and that the whole position is still quite inconclusive. One of the reasons for this state of affairs is the present uncertainty about the validity of psycho-analytic method. Because of the doubts about it, we are uncertain what weight to attach to a theory that is based primarily on the data that the method provides. But, of course, *all* psycho-analytic and cognate theories are in the same boat in this respect. Insofar as they rely on psycho-analytic method in some form, they are all of uncertain weight. Given, however, the weakness of all these theories, are there any rational grounds for accepting one of them rather than another – for accepting, say, a Freudian rather than a Jungian scheme? Accordingly, are there any further rational grounds for accepting the Freudian narrative about Leonardo rather than a Jungian one? The short answer is that there are rational grounds available to aid in a decision here, but these are far from being sufficient to settle matters conclusively and to obtain a general consensus. Thus, we can appeal to the simplicity of a particular psycho-analytic theory or scheme in contrast with another; its greater plausibility in the light of biological knowledge and current trends in medicine; its greater clarity; its wider scope and greater power, or richness, in generating clinical expectancies. But these criteria or considerations are not good enough, severally or jointly, to settle matters. For they only work well when the theories concerned are sufficiently developed and constructed to allow the criteria to be clearly and decisively applied. The typical theories, however, in the field we are dealing with are so poorly developed and constructed that the attempt to apply these criteria, far from settling matters, is apt to generate further heat and dissension.

But, naturally enough, a worker in this field usually does make some sort of decision about these psycho-analytic theories for purely pragmatic reasons. He has to handle the materials that the theories are concerned with; and he finds it practically necessary to take some personal stand about them. This decision, however, is largely the outcome of non-rational considerations. The particular stand he takes will depend on things such as his own philosophical position in respect of mind and science, and the sort of language he prefers to talk; the sort of personal psycho-analysis he has had if any; and, more subtly, the influence on him of his own self-analysis. This last is important, since no technical worker in this field can avoid self-analysis in some measure. If, in the course of this analysis, he has been trapped into using one particular psycho-analytic theory on himself, he will be moved to regard this theory as getting at something authentic and important, and better than an alternative theory that he has not found personally helpful.

What is more, the ordinary educated person is also under a little pressure today to take some sort of stand about these alternative theories in the field of personality and psycho-analysis. If he succumbs to this pressure, he too will be influenced by non-rational considerations. In particular, he is likely to be influenced by the personal impact that Freud and others make on him. His reading of psycho-analytical writings will set going some self-analysis; and if he finds some particular theory personally disturbing and illuminating, in whole or part, he will be moved to regard this theory as better than an alternative which does not disturb and illuminate. When, therefore, technical workers and the ordinary person consider the theory embodied in Freud's essay on Leonardo, there is a great deal of room for rational discussion about the merits of the theory and how it compares with alternatives. But a point may be reached when the perceptive among us will recognize that the intellectual conflict about these theories and theoretical preferences is being maintained by non-rational considerations. At this point, we can only take note that these are at work, accept and respect them, and pass on.

10

When we sought to understand our new next-door neighbour, we were in search of a narrative about him which removed the inconsistencies he presented, and which was true. In seeking to understand Leonardo, Freud has tried to give us a narrative of the same sort – one which removes the inconsistencies in his life and work, and which is true. How successful was Freud in this attempt?

It is reasonable to claim that Freud's narrative does seem to remove the inconsistencies fairly well, and to present a story about Leonardo which is coherent and which offers a good coverage of the data. But is it true? Clearly there are some reasons for thinking that, in its main outline, it *may* be true; and some reasons for thinking that parts of the narrative are stronger than others. Because it is apparently coherent, offers good coverage, and may be true, it does throw some light into the darkness surrounding Leonardo, and does do something to dispel the enigma he presents. However, it is also abundantly clear that we have little, if any, reason to believe, or to claim to know, that Freud's narrative *is* true. We are not logically obliged to accept it. What is more, our examination of Freud's narrative suggests that we are not logically obliged to accept *any* all-embracing narrative about Leonardo at the present time. There appears to be no alternative candidate in the field which compels our allegiance either.

What, then, shall we do when we are asked to resolve the enigma of Leonardo – to make him understandable? Shall we say that, as Freud's story or any of the current alternatives is not obligatory for us but is more or less inadequate, we shall refuse to spin *any* of them? Shall we, in other words, just decline for these reasons to offer any all-embracing narrative about Leonardo? Or shall we say that, inadequate though all these narratives are, we shall make use of one or more of them in order to throw what light they can on the puzzle that Leonardo presents? Neither choice is free from difficulties. If we take the former alternative, we lay ourselves open to the charge of being unreasonable. For we are overlooking the help that Freud's narrative, as well as the others, can give us; and we are, in a way, just revealing our personal decision only to use a narrative that we believe or know to be true. If we choose the latter alternative, we shall have to be careful to use our narrative, or narratives, with care. We must guard against falling in love with the one we happen to find most congenial, and, ideally, we should go out of our way to use several narratives to describe Leonardo, in order thereby to bring out their comparative strength and weakness.

The choice we make here is apt to be closely connected with the educational and professional background we bring with us. If we come to Freud's essay from the physical sciences, or experimental psychology, or the so-called 'objective' study of personality, or an 'objective' clinical psychology, or from an organically oriented psychiatry, or neurology and brain surgery – if we come to the essay from these and similar directions, we are likely to view Freud's story about Leonardo (or any alternative) with great scepticism. We will probably be disinclined to take it at all seriously. On the other hand, if we approach the essay from history or literature, or as a teacher from an eclectic background in psychology, or from functional or dynamic psychiatry – if we approach the essay from these directions, we will probably receive it favourably, and we will be ready to try to explain Leonardo by means of it, or some alternative. The choice we make here is apt to be connected with our educational and professional background for the following reason. If our professional training has been in, let us suppose, one of the physical sciences, or in experimental or objective psychology, we will have learned to use and operate with what can be called 'a certain level of satisfactory proof'. It is by reference to this level that we distinguish in our own specialism between narratives that are rationally acceptable and those that are not. When, then, we come to Freud's essay from such a direction, we will be apt to bring this level of satisfactory proof with us, and to judge the essay in terms of it. Now this particular level is a high one, and the essay completely fails to reach it. Hence we refuse to touch the essay. We regard it with scepticism and decline to take it seriously. In contrast, if our professional training has been in, say, literature, the level of satisfactory proof which we will have to use will be rather different from, and often lower than, the one we would acquire in the physical sciences. For instance, if we offer an account of Wordsworth's character, the requirements that our narrative will have to satisfy to be rationally acceptable will be less strict and severe than those typical of natural science. Consequently, when we come upon Freud's narrative, we will judge it in terms of a level of rational acceptability, or satisfactory proof, that is much closer to the one Freud himself employed. We will be disposed for this reason to receive it favourably and seriously. Therefore, if we judge the essay in terms of a high level of satisfactory proof, we will reject it, and any current alternative, as unproven. If we judge the essay in terms of a lower level of proof, we may decide that Freud's narrative, or some alternative, inadequate though it is, is good enough to use to throw light on the enigma of Leonardo. But whatever we choose to do, both courses run us into difficulties. If we refuse to use any of these narratives, we meet the objection that we are really only doing concealed propaganda for our own high level of proof, and are just being inflexibly impervious to the subtleties of the conceptual situation. If we are ready to use these narratives, we have to use them with a care and detachment that it is difficult for us to achieve and maintain.

However, whether we accept Freud's essay as unproven, or are prepared to use it, in part or whole, at a lower level of acceptability, there is one thing on which there seems to be general agreement. This is the enormous stimulus that the essay has given to critics and historians of art in their attempts to understand Leonardo. Moreover, the essay also seems to have helped, along with the rest of the Freudian corpus, to transform their general attitude to human nature, and to the work of the artist. This transformation may or may not be justified. But it seems to be a fact, and one that has been stressed in recent years. On the other hand, it also seems to be a fact that the essay has not given much stimulus to the historians of science – in their study either of Leonardo or of creative scientific work in general. Why the essay has failed here, and whether this failure is justified are interesting questions which, perhaps, the historians of science should try to answer.

The influence of the essay on the psychological world has not been large; and at the present time the attitude to it seems to be somewhat uncertain. Psychiatrists, psychotherapists, psychologists of personality, and even analysts themselves will be inclined to see in the essay an intriguing, courageous, but untypical exercise in the application of Freudian theory of the middle period. But they will also be inclined to regard it as having only a historical interest at the present time. To these often hardheaded people, many of them overworked in the day-to-day struggle to improve the mental health of their patients, the study of Freud's essay may seem to be just a piece of antiquarian research with no practical relevance whatever. 'What on earth does it matter if Freud was right in supposing that Leonardo remained with Caterina for some years? Or if he and Reitler were wrong about the coition figure?' But this reaction is a mistake. Far from the essay being only a matter of historical interest, it has some contemporary and practical relevance.

It is a fact, no doubt harsh and unwelcome, that psychiatrists, analysts, psychotherapists, and others of this genus, do not yet enjoy a respectable status in the world of science and learning. They have not yet been accepted by their fellow-doctors, psychologists, and others as reputable partners in a joint enterprise. One of the sources of this state of affairs lies in the nature of their work. This work constitutes one of the most perplexing branches of modern science and medicine. An essential and large part of it consists in the attempt to diagnose and treat mental disorders; and an essential part, in turn, of this effort lies in the production and use of interpretations and interpretative narratives about a patient. At the present time, confusion seems to be fairly widespread about the nature of the whole attempt to diagnose and treat, and, in particular, about the character of the interpretations and interpretative narratives used in this work. The problem is complicated by the fact that the material concerned is often private and non-reproducible, complex and evanescent. Obviously it is highly desirable to dispel – as much and as soon as we can – the confusion and uncertainty that surrounds this whole enterprise on behalf of mental health.

Now when we are faced by a complicated problem, one of the recognized ways of opening it up is to consider it in some simplified form. We consider some situation, or condition, or what not, which is simpler than the one our problem is really concerned with, and yet which is relevantly analogous to the situation our problem is about. As it is a simpler situation, we can get to grips with it; as it is relevantly analogous to the one we are really concerned about, we will be able to generalize our results from the simplified situation we have examined to the more complex one we are really interested in. The value of this procedure depends largely on our success in hitting upon a simplified situation which is such that we can investigate it successfully with whatever methods we have at our disposal, and which is relevantly analogous to the one that really concerns us. This procedure, of course, is characteristic of scientific work. It is also, interestingly enough, one of the devices philosophers have learned from Wittgenstein. When philosophers wish to investigate a problem that involves the use of complicated concepts, they sometimes proceed to think of, or imagine, a situation where the concepts and the language they are concerned with can be studied in a simplified form.

What Freud has given us in this essay on Leonardo is a simplified case study. He has asked us to consider a narrative that is less complex than those usually presented by psychiatrists, analysts, and others about a patient. It is less complex in various ways. The data on which the narrative is based contain no material from psycho-analytic sessions, and so the narrative is free from the uncertainty that – as we saw – comes with material from this source. The data concerned are public, acceptable, and fixed by the historical record. Moreover, Freud's narrative, unlike the usual one about a patient, is good enough to reveal that it contains clear-cut mistakes – interpretations that are false. Yet, in a number of relevant respects, his narrative is very like the usual, full story that analysts and others produce about a patient. By examining it, therefore, we are able to get to grips with the complicated problem presented by the narratives used in the diagnosis and treatment of mental disorder. We can use Freud's essay to help us in our efforts to clear up and dispel the confusion that surrounds this work. The essay, therefore, is certainly not of historical interest alone, and the examination of it is far from being just a piece of antiquarian research.

In our study of the essay we have attempted to deal with the doubts and difficulties that the ordinary person is likely to have about it. We have tried, in particular, to make clear what credence we can attach to the essay as a whole and to various parts of it. In the course of doing this, we have also done something to exhibit the character of the sort of interpretative narrative that is central to the activity of many psychiatrists, analysts, and others. We have shown something of the rationale of this sort of narrative, and something of its difficulties, where it is reasonable and can make a contribution, and where its limitations are to be found. Whatever we may think of the value of Freud's attempt to understand Leonardo – whatever we may decide about the substantive answer he provides – we must be grateful to him for his genius and audacity in giving us this simplified case study of Leonardo. By means of it he has thrown light on the nature of the discourse we use about mental disorder, and helped to resolve some of the problems it generates. For this we are all in his debt.

LEONARDO

ONE

WHEN psychiatric research, normally content to draw on frailer men for its material, approaches one who is among the greatest of the human race, it is not doing so for the reasons so frequently ascribed to it by laymen. 'To blacken the radiant and drag the sublime into the dust' is no part of its purpose,[1] and there is no satisfaction for it in narrowing the gulf which separates the perfection of the great from the inadequacy of the objects that are its usual concern. But it cannot help finding worthy of understanding everything that can be recognized in those illustrious models, and it believes there is no one so great as to be disgraced by being subject to the laws which govern both normal and pathological activity with equal cogency.

Leonardo da Vinci (1452–1519) was admired even by his contemporaries as one of the greatest men of the Italian renaissance; yet in their time he had already begun to seem an enigma, just as he does to us today. He was a universal genius 'whose outlines can only be surmised, never defined'.[2] In his own time his most decisive influence was in painting, and it was left to us to recognize the greatness of the natural scientist (and

1. [*Es liebt die Welt, das Strahlende zu schwärzen*
       Und das Erhabene in den Staub zu ziehn.

(The world loves to blacken the radiant and drag the sublime into the dust.)

From a poem by Schiller, *Das Mädchen von Orleans*, inserted as an extra prologue to the 1801 edition of his play *Die Jungfrau von Orleans*. The poem is reputed to have been an attack on Voltaire's *La Pucelle*.]

2. The words are Jacob Burckhardt's, quoted by Konstantinowa (1907, [51]).

engineer)[1] that was combined in him with the artist. Though he left behind him masterpieces of painting, while his scientific discoveries remained unpublished and unused, the investigator in him never in the course of his development left the artist entirely free, but often made severe encroachments on him and perhaps in the end suppressed him. In the last hour of his life, according to the words that Vasari gives him, he reproached himself with having offended God and man by his failure to do his duty in his art.[2] And even if this story of Vasari's has neither external nor much internal probability but belongs to the legend which began to be woven around the mysterious Master even before his death, it is still of incontestable value as evidence of what men believed at the time.

What was it that prevented Leonardo's personality from being understood by his contemporaries? The cause of this was certainly not the versatility of his talents and the range of his knowledge, which enabled him to introduce himself to the court of the Duke of Milan, Lodovico Sforza, called Il Moro, as a performer on a kind of lute of his own invention, or allowed him to write the remarkable letter to the same duke in which he boasted of his achievements as architect and military engineer. For the days of the renaissance were quite familiar with such a combination of wide and diverse abilities in a single individual – though we must allow that Leonardo himself was one of the most bril-

1. [The words in parentheses were added in 1923.]
2. '*Egli per reverenza, rizzatosi a sedere sul letto, contando il mal suo e gli accidenti di quello, mostrava tuttavia quanto avea offeso Dio e gli uomini del mondo, non avendo operato nell'arte come si conveniva.*' ['He having raised himself out of reverence so as to sit on the bed, and giving an account of his illness and its circumstances, yet showed how much he had offended God and mankind in not having worked at his art as he should have done.'] Vasari [ed. Poggi (1919, 43)].

liant examples of this. Nor did he belong to the type of
genius who has received a niggardly outward endow-
ment from Nature, and who in his turn places no value
on the outward forms of life, but in a spirit of painful
gloom flies from all dealings with mankind. On the
contrary, he was tall and well-proportioned; his features were of consummate beauty and his physical
strength unusual; he was charming in his manner,
supremely eloquent, and cheerful and amiable to everyone. He loved beauty in the things that surrounded
him; he was fond of magnificent clothing and valued
every refinement of living. In a passage from the treatise
on painting, which reveals his lively capacity for enjoyment, he compares painting with its sister arts and
describes the hardships that await the sculptor: 'For
his face is smeared and dusted all over with marble
powder so that he looks like a baker, and he is completely covered with little chips of marble, so that it
seems as if his back had been snowed on; and his house
is full of splinters of stone and dust. In the case of the
painter it is quite different ... for the painter sits in
front of his work in perfect comfort. He is well-dressed
and handles the lightest of brushes which he dips in
pleasant colours. He wears the clothes he likes; and his
house is full of delightful paintings, and is spotlessly
clean. He is often accompanied by music or by men
who read from a variety of beautiful works, and he can
listen to these with great pleasure and without the din
of hammers and other noises.'[1]

It is indeed quite possible that the idea of a radiantly
happy and pleasure-loving Leonardo is only applicable
to the first and longer period of the artist's life. Afterwards, when the downfall of Lodovico Moro's rule

1. *Trattato della Pittura* [Ludwig (1909, 36); also Richter, I. A.
(1952, 33of.)].

forced him to leave Milan, the city that was the centre of his activity and where his position was assured, and to pursue a life lacking in security and not rich in external successes, until he found his last asylum in France, the sparkle of his temperament may have grown dim and some strange sides of his nature may have been thrown into prominence. Moreover the turning of his interests from his art to science, which increased as time went on, must have played its part in widening the gulf between himself and his contemporaries. All the efforts in which in their opinion he frittered away his time when he could have been industriously painting to order and becoming rich (as, for example, his former fellow-student Perugino did) seemed to them to be merely capricious trifling or even caused him to be suspected of being in the service of the 'black art'. We are in a position to understand him better, for we know from his notes what were the arts that he practised. In an age which was beginning to replace the authority of the Church by that of antiquity and which was not yet familiar with any form of research not based on presuppositions, Leonardo – the forerunner and by no means unworthy rival of Bacon and Copernicus – was necessarily isolated. In his dissection of the dead bodies of horses and human beings, in his construction of flying machines, and in his studies on the nutrition of plants and their reactions to poisons, he certainly departed widely from the commentators on Aristotle, and came close to the despised alchemists, in whose laboratories experimental research had found some refuge at least in those unfavourable times.

The effect that this had on his painting was that he took up his brush with reluctance, painted less and less, left what he had begun for the most part unfinished and cared little about the ultimate fate of his works. And this was what he was blamed for by his contemporaries: to them his attitude towards his art remained a riddle.

Several of Leonardo's later admirers have made attempts to acquit his character of the flaw of instability. In his defence they claim that he is blamed for what is a general feature of great artists: even the energetic Michelangelo, a man entirely given up to his labours, left many of his works incomplete, and it was no more his fault than it was Leonardo's in the parallel instance. Moreover, in the case of some of the pictures, they urge, it is not so much a question of their being unfinished as of his declaring them to be so. What appears to the layman as a masterpiece is never for the creator of the work of art more than an unsatisfactory embodiment of what he intended; he has some dim notion of a perfection, whose likeness time and again he despairs of reproducing. Least of all, they claim, is it right to make the artist responsible for the ultimate fate of his works.

Valid as some of these excuses may be, they still do not cover the whole state of affairs that confronts us in Leonardo. The same distressing struggle with a work, the final flight from it and the indifference to its future fate may recur in many other artists, but there is no doubt that this behaviour is shown in Leonardo in an extreme degree. Solmi (1910, 12) quotes the remark of one of his pupils: *'Pareva che ad ogni ora tremasse, quando si poneva a dipingere, e però non diede mai fine ad alcuna cosa cominciata, considerando la grandezza dell'arte, tal che egli scorgeva errori in quelle cose, che ad altri parevano miracoli.'*[1] His last pictures, he goes on, the 'Leda', the 'Madonna

1. ['He appeared to tremble the whole time when he set himself to paint, and yet he never completed any work he had begun, having so high a regard for the greatness of art that he discovered faults in things that to others seemed miracles.']

di Sant' Onofrio', 'Bacchus', and the young 'St John
the Baptist', remained unfinished '*come quasi intervenne di
tutte le cose sue . . .*'[1] Lomazzo, who made a copy of the
'Last Supper', refers in a sonnet to Leonardo's notorious inability to finish his works:

> *Protogen che il pennel di sue pitture*
> *Non levava, agguaglio il Vinci Divo*
> *Di cui opra non è finita pure.*[2]

The slowness with which Leonardo worked was
proverbial. He painted at the 'Last Supper' in the
Convent of Santa Maria delle Grazie in Milan, after
the most thorough preparatory studies, for three whole
years. One of his contemporaries, Matteo Bandelli, the
story-writer, who at the time was a young monk in the
convent, tells how Leonardo often used to climb up the
scaffolding early in the morning and remain there till
twilight never once laying his brush aside, and with no
thought of eating or drinking. Then days would pass
without his putting his hand to it. Sometimes he would
remain for hours in front of the painting, merely examining it in his mind. At other times he would come
straight to the convent from the court in the castle at
Milan, where he was making the model of the equestrian
statue for Francesco Sforza, in order to add a few strokes
of the brush to a figure, and then immediately break
off.[3] According to Vasari he spent four years in painting
the portrait of Mona Lisa, the wife of the Florentine
Francesco del Giocondo, without being able to bring it

---

1. ['As happened more or less to all his works.']

2. ['Protogenes, who never lifted his brush from his work, was
the equal of the divine Vinci, who never finished anything at all.']
Quoted by Scognamiglio (1900, [112]).

3. Von Seidlitz (1909, **1**, 203).

to final completion. This circumstance may also account for the fact that the picture was never delivered to the man who commissioned it, but instead remained with Leonardo and was taken to France by him.[1] It was bought by King Francis I, and today forms one of the greatest treasures of the Louvre.

If these reports of the way in which Leonardo worked are compared with the evidence of the extraordinarily numerous sketches and studies which he left behind him and which exhibit every *motif* appearing in his paintings in a great variety of forms, we are bound totally to reject the idea that traits of hastiness and unsteadiness acquired the slightest influence over Leonardo's relation to his art. On the contrary, it is possible to observe a quite extraordinary profundity, a wealth of possibilities between which a decision can only be reached with hesitation, demands which can hardly be satisfied, and an inhibition in the actual execution which is not in fact to be explained even by the artist inevitably falling short of his ideal. The slowness which had all along been conspicuous in Leonardo's work is seen to be a symptom of this inhibition and to be the forerunner of his subsequent withdrawal from painting.[2] It was this too which determined the fate of the 'Last Supper' – a fate that was not undeserved. Leonardo could not become reconciled to fresco painting, which demands rapid work while the ground is still moist, and this was the reason why he chose oil colours, the drying of which permitted him to protract the completion of the painting to suit his mood and leisure. These pigments however detached themselves from the ground on which they were applied and which separated them from the

1. Von Seidlitz (1909, **2**, 48).
2. Pater [1873, 100]: 'But it is certain that at one period of his life he had almost ceased to be an artist.'

wall. Added to this, the defects in the wall, and the later fortunes of the building itself, determined what seems to be the inevitable ruin of the picture.[1]

The miscarriage of a similar technical experiment appears to have caused the destruction of the 'Battle of Anghiari', the painting which, in competition with Michelangelo, he began to paint some time afterwards on a wall of the Sala del Consiglio in Florence, and which he also abandoned in an unfinished condition. Here it seems as if an alien interest – in experimentation – at first reinforced the artistic one, only to damage the work later on.

The character of Leonardo the man showed some other unusual traits and apparent contradictions. A certain inactivity and indifference seemed obvious to him. At a time when everyone was trying to gain the widest scope for his activity – a goal unattainable without the development of energetic aggressiveness towards other people – Leonardo was notable for his quiet peaceableness and his avoidance of all antagonism and controversy. He was gentle and kindly to everyone; he declined, it is said, to eat meat, since he did not think it justifiable to deprive animals of their lives; and he took particular pleasure in buying birds in the market and setting them free.[2] He condemned war and bloodshed and described man as not so much the king of the animal world but rather the worst of the wild beasts.[3] But this feminine delicacy of feeling did not deter him

1. See von Seidlitz (1909, 1, [205 ff.]) for the history of the attempts to restore and preserve the picture.

2. Müntz (1899, 18). A letter of a contemporary from India to one of the Medici alludes to this characteristic behaviour of Leonardo. (See J. P. Richter [1939, 2, 103–4n.].)

3. Bottazzi (1910, 186).

LEONARDO

from accompanying condemned criminals on their way to execution in order to study their features distorted by fear and to sketch them in his notebook. Nor did it stop him from devising the cruellest offensive weapons and from entering the service of Cesare Borgia as chief military engineer. He often gave the appearance of being indifferent to good and evil, or he insisted on measurement by a special standard. He accompanied Cesare in a position of authority during the campaign that brought the Romagna into the possession of that most ruthless and faithless of adversaries. There is not a line in Leonardo's notebooks which reveals any criticism of the events of those days, or any concern in them. A comparison suggests itself here with Goethe during the French campaign.

If a biographical study is really intended to arrive at an understanding of its hero's mental life it must not – as happens in the majority of biographies as a result of discretion or prudishness – silently pass over its subject's sexual activity or sexual individuality. What is known of Leonardo in this respect is little: but that little is full of significance. In an age which saw a struggle between sensuality without restraint and gloomy asceticism, Leonardo represented the cool repudiation of sexuality – a thing that would scarcely be expected of an artist and a portrayer of feminine beauty. Solmi quotes the following sentence of his which is evidence of his frigidity: 'The act of procreation and everything connected with it is so disgusting that mankind would soon die out if it were not an old-established custom and if there were not pretty faces and sensuous natures.'[1] His posthumous writings, which not only deal with the greatest scientific problems but also contain trivialities that strike us as scarcely worthy of so great a mind (an

1. Solmi (1908, [24]).

99

allegorical natural history, animal fables, jokes, prophecies),[1] are chaste – one might say even abstinent – to a degree that would cause surprise in a work of *belles lettres* even today. So resolutely do they shun everything sexual that it would seem as if Eros alone, the preserver of all living things, was not worthy material for the investigator in his pursuit of knowledge.[2] It is well known how frequently great artists take pleasure in giving vent to their phantasies in erotic and even crudely obscene pictures. In Leonardo's case on the contrary we have only some anatomical sketches of the internal female genitals, the position of the embryo in the womb, and so on.[3]

1. Herzfeld (1906).

2. An exception to this (though an unimportant one) is perhaps to be found in his collected witticisms – *belle facezie* – which have not been translated. See Herzfeld (1906, 151). [This reference to Eros as 'the preserver of all living things' seems to anticipate Freud's introduction of the name ten years later, in almost exactly the same phrase, as a general term for the sexual as opposed to the death instincts. See, for instance, *Beyond the Pleasure Principle* (1920*b*), *Standard Ed.*, **18**, 50 and 52.]

3. [*Footnote added* 1919:] Some remarkable errors are visible in a drawing made by Leonardo of the sexual act seen in anatomical sagittal section, which certainly cannot be called obscene. They were discovered by Reitler (1917) and discussed by him in the light of the account which I have given here of Leonardo's character:

'It is precisely in the process of portraying the act of procreation that this excessive instinct for research has totally failed – obviously only as a result of his even greater sexual repression. The man's body is drawn in full, the woman's only in part. If the drawing reproduced in Fig. 1 is shown to an unprejudiced onlooker with the head visible but all the lower parts covered up, it may be safely assumed that the head will be taken to be a woman's. The wavy locks on the forehead, and the others, which flow down the back approximately to the fourth or fifth dorsal vertebra, mark the head as more of a woman's than a man's.

It is doubtful whether Leonardo ever embraced a woman in passion; nor is it known that he had any intimate mental relationship with a woman, such as

---

'The woman's breast reveals two defects. The first indeed is an artistic one, for its outline gives it the appearance of a breast that is flabby and hangs down unpleasingly. The second defect is anatomical, for Leonardo the researcher had obviously been prevented by his fending off of sexuality from ever making a close examination of a nursing woman's nipples. Had he done so he would have been bound to notice that the milk flows out of a number of separate excretory ducts. Leonardo, however, drew only a single duct extending far down into the abdominal cavity and probably in his view drawing the milk from the *cisterna chyli* and perhaps also connected in some way with the sex organs. It must of course be taken into consideration that the study of the internal organs of the human body was at that time made extremely difficult, since the dissection of bodies was regarded as desecration of the dead and was most severely punished. Whether Leonardo, who had certainly only very little material for dissection at his disposal, knew anything at all of the existence of a lymph-reservoir in the abdominal cavity is therefore in fact highly questionable, although in his drawing he included a cavity that is no doubt intended to be something of the sort. But from his making the lactiferous duct extend still further downwards till it reaches the internal sex organs we may suspect that he was trying to represent the synchronization of the beginning of the secretion of milk and the end of pregnancy by means of visible anatomical connexions as well. However, even if we are ready to excuse the artist's defective knowledge of anatomy by referring it to the circumstances of his time, the striking fact still remains that it is precisely the female genital that Leonardo has treated so carelessly. The vagina and something that looks like the *portio uteri* can no doubt be made out, but the lines indicating the uterus itself are completely confused.

'The male genital on the other hand is depicted by Leonardo much more correctly. Thus, for instance, he was not satisfied with drawing the testis but also put in the epididymis, which he drew with perfect accuracy.

'What is especially remarkable is the posture in which Leonardo

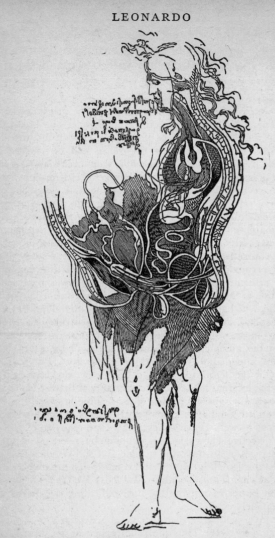

FIG. I. Wehrt's version of the Leonardo coition figure, obtained by copying the inaccurate engraving of Bartolozzi, and assumed by Freud to be authentic.

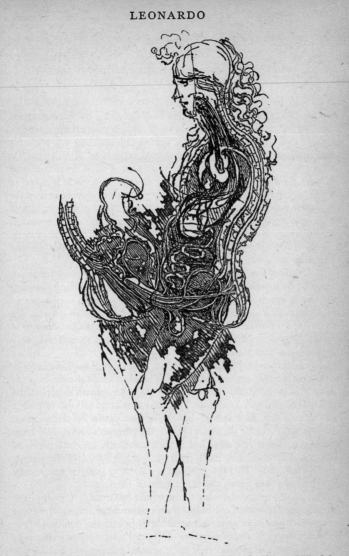

FIG. 2. Leonardo's coition figure (*Quad. Anat.* III fol.
3 v., copyright reserved).

Michelangelo's with Vittoria Colonna. While he was still an apprentice, living in the house of his master Verrocchio, a charge of forbidden homosexual prac-

---

makes coitus take place. Pictures and drawings by famous artists exist which depict *coitus a tergo, a latere*, etc., but when it comes to a drawing of the sexual act being performed standing up, we must surely suppose that there was a sexual repression of quite special strength to have caused it to be represented in this isolated and almost grotesque way. If one wants to enjoy oneself it is usual to make oneself as comfortable as possible: this of course is true for both the primal instincts, hunger and love. Most of the peoples of antiquity took their meals in a lying position and it is normal in coitus today to lie down just as comfortably as did our ancestors. Lying down implies more or less a wish to stay in the desired situation for some time.

'Moreover the features of the man with the feminine head are marked by a resistance that is positively indignant. His brows are wrinkled and his gaze is directed sideways with an expression of repugnance. The lips are pressed together and their corners are then drawn down. In this face can be seen neither the pleasure of love's blessings nor the happiness of indulgence: it expresses only indignation and aversion.

'The clumsiest blunder, however, was made by Leonardo in drawing the two lower extremities. The man's foot should in point of fact have been his right one; for since Leonardo depicted the act of union in an anatomical sagittal section it follows of course the man's left foot would be above the plane of the picture. Conversely, and for the same reason, the woman's foot should have belonged to her left side. But in fact Leonardo has interchanged male and female. The male figure has a left foot and the female one a right foot. This interchange is easiest to grasp if one recalls that the big toes lie on the inner sides of the feet.

'This anatomical drawing alone would have made it possible to deduce the repression of libido – a repression which threw the great artist and investigator into something approaching confusion.'

[*Added* 1923:] These remarks of Reitler's have been criticized, it is true, on the ground that such serious conclusions should not be drawn from a hasty sketch, and that it is not even certain whether the different parts of the drawing really belong together.

tices was brought against him, along with some other young people, which ended in his acquittal. He seems to have fallen under this suspicion because he had employed a boy of bad reputation as a model.[1] When he had become a Master, he surrounded himself with handsome boys and youths whom he took as pupils. The last of these pupils, Francesco Melzi, accompanied him to France, remained with him up to his death, and was named by him as his heir. Without sharing in the certainty of his modern biographers, who naturally reject the possibility that there was a sexual relationship between him and his pupils as a baseless insult to the great man, we may take it as much more probable that Leonardo's affectionate relations with the young men who – as was the custom with pupils at that time – shared his existence did not extend to sexual activity. Moreover a high degree of sexual activity is not to be attributed to him.

There is only one way in which the peculiarity of this emotional and sexual life can be understood in connexion with Leonardo's double nature as an artist and as a scientific investigator. Among his biographers, to whom a psychological approach is often very alien, there is to my knowledge only one, Edmondo Solmi, who has approached the solution of the problem; but a writer who has chosen Leonardo as the hero of a great historical novel, Dmitry Sergeyevich Merezhkovsky, has made a similar reading of this unusual man the basis of his portrait and has given clear expression to his con-

1. According to Scognamiglio (1900, 49) there is a reference to this episode in an obscure and even variously read passage in the *Codex Atlanticus*: '*Quando io feci Domeneddio putto voi mi metteste in prigione, ora s'io lo fo grande, voi mi farete peggio.*' ['When I represented the Lord God as a baby, you put me in prison; now if I represent him as an adult you will do worse to me.']

ception, not indeed in plain language, but (after the way of writers of imagination) in plastic terms.[1] Solmi's verdict on Leonardo is as follows (1908, 46): 'But his insatiable desire to understand everything around him, and to fathom in a spirit of cold superiority the deepest secret of all that is perfect, had condemned Leonardo's work to remain for ever unfinished.'

In an essay in the *Conferenze Fiorentine* the following pronouncement of Leonardo's is quoted, which represents his confession of faith and provides the key to his nature: *'Nessuna cosa si può amare nè odiare, se prima non si ha cognition di quella.'*[2] That is to say: One has no right to love or hate anything if one has not acquired a thorough knowledge of its nature. And the same is repeated by Leonardo in a passage in the treatise on painting where he seems to be defending himself against the charge of irreligion: 'But such carping critics would do better to keep silent. For that (line of conduct) is the way to become acquainted with the Creator of so many wonderful things, and this is the way to love so great an Inventor. For in truth great love springs from great knowledge of the beloved object, and if you know it but little you will be able to love it only a little or not at all . . .'[3]

The value of these remarks of Leonardo's is not to be looked for in their conveying an important psychological fact; for what they assert is obviously false, and Leonardo must have known this as well as we do. It is not true that human beings delay loving or hating until

1. Merezhkovsky, 1902; German trans., 1903. *Leonardo da Vinci* forms the second work of a great historical trilogy entitled *Christ and Antichrist*. The two other volumes are *Julian the Apostate* and *Peter and Alexis.*
2. Bottazzi (1910, 193) [J. P. Richter (1939, 2, 244)].
3. *Trattato della Pittura* [Ludwig (1909, 54)].

they have studied and become familiar with the nature of the object to which these affects apply. On the contrary they love impulsively, from emotional motives which have nothing to do with knowledge, and whose operation is at most weakened by reflection and consideration. Leonardo, then, could only have meant that the love practised by human beings was not of the proper and unobjectionable kind: one *should* love in such a way as to hold back the affect, subject it to the process of reflection, and only let it take its course when it has stood up to the test of thought. And at the same time we understand that he wishes to tell us that it happens so in his case and that it would be worth while for everyone else to treat love and hatred as he does.

And in his case it really seems to have been so. His affects were controlled and subjected to the instinct for research; he did not love and hate, but asked himself about the origin and significance of what he was to love or hate. Thus he was bound at first to appear indifferent to good and evil, beauty and ugliness. During this work of investigation love and hate threw off their positive or negative signs and were both alike transformed into intellectual interest. In reality Leonardo was not devoid of passion; he did not lack the divine spark which is directly or indirectly the driving force – *il primo motore* – behind all human activity. He had merely converted his passion into a thirst for knowledge; he then applied himself to investigation with the persistence, constancy, and penetration which is derived from passion, and at the climax of intellectual labour, when knowledge had been won, he allowed the long restrained affect to break loose and to flow away freely, as a stream of water drawn from a river is allowed to flow away when its work is done. When, at the climax of a discovery, he could survey a large portion of the whole nexus, he was overcome by emotion, and in ecstatic language praised the splendour of the part of creation that he had studied, or – in religious phraseology – the greatness of his Creator. This process of transformation in Leonardo has been rightly understood by Solmi. After quoting a passage of this sort in which Leonardo celebrates the sublime law of nature ('*O mirabile necessità . . .*'), he writes (1910, 11): '*Tale trasfigurazione della scienza della natura in emozione, quasi direi, religiosa, è uno dei tratti caratteristici de' manoscritti vinciani, e si trova cento e cento volte espressa. . . .*'[1]

Because of his insatiable and indefatigable thirst for knowledge Leonardo has been called the Italian Faust. But quite apart from doubts about a possible transformation of the instinct to investigate back into an enjoyment of life – a transformation which we must take as fundamental in the tragedy of Faust – the view may be hazarded that Leonardo's development approaches Spinoza's mode of thinking.

A conversion of psychical instinctual force into various forms of activity can perhaps no more be achieved without loss than a conversion of physical forces. The example of Leonardo teaches us how many other things we have to take into account in connexion with these processes. The postponement of loving until full knowledge is acquired ends in a substitution of the latter for the former. A man who has won his way to a state of knowledge cannot properly be said to love and hate; he remains beyond love and hatred. He has investigated instead of loving. And that is perhaps why Leonardo's life was so much poorer in love than that of other great men, and of other artists. The stormy passions

1. ['Such a transfiguration of natural science into a sort of religious emotion is one of the characteristic features of Leonardo's manuscripts, and there are hundreds and hundreds of examples of it.']

of a nature that inspires and consumes, passions in which other men have enjoyed their richest experience, appear not to have touched him.

There are some further consequences. Investigating has taken the place of acting and creating as well. A man who has begun to have an inkling of the grandeur of the universe with all its complexities and its laws readily forgets his own insignificant self. Lost in admiration and filled with true humility, he all too easily forgets that he himself is a part of those active forces and that in accordance with the scale of his personal strength the way is open for him to try to alter a small portion of the destined course of the world – a world in which the small is still no less wonderful and significant than the great.

Leonardo's researches had perhaps first begun, as Solmi believes, in the service of his art;[1] he directed his efforts to the properties and laws of light, colours, shadows, and perspective in order to ensure mastery in the imitation of nature and to point the same way to others. It is probable that at that time he already over-rated the value to the artist of these branches of knowledge. Still constantly following the lead given by the requirements of his painting he was then driven to investigate the painter's subjects, animals and plants and the proportions of the human body, and, passing from their exterior, to proceed to gain a knowledge of their internal structure and their vital functions, which indeed also find expression in their appearance and

1. Solmi (1910, 8): '*Leonardo aveva posto, come regola al pittore, lo studio della natura . . . poi la passione dello studio era divenuta dominante egli aveva voluto acquistare non più la scienza per l'arte, ma la scienza per la scienza.*' ['Leonardo had prescribed the study of nature as a rule for the painter . . . then the passion for study had become dominant, he had no longer wished to acquire learning for the sake of art, but learning for the sake of learning.']

have a claim to be depicted in art. And finally the instinct, which had become overwhelming, swept him away until the connexion with the demands of his art was severed, so that he discovered the general laws of mechanics and divined the history of the stratification and fossilization in the Arno valley, and until he could enter in large letters in his book the discovery: *Il sole non si move*.[1] His investigations extended to practically every branch of natural science, and in every single one he was a discoverer or at least a prophet and pioneer.[2] Yet his urge for knowledge was always directed to the external world; something kept him far away from the investigation of the human mind. In the 'Academia Vinciana' [p. 174], for which he drew some cleverly intertwined emblems, there was little room for psychology.

Then, when he made the attempt to return from investigation to his starting-point, the exercise of his art, he found himself disturbed by the new direction of his interests and the changed nature of his mental activity. What interested him in a picture was above all a problem; and behind the first one he saw countless other problems arising, just as he used to in his endless and inexhaustible investigation of nature. He was no longer able to limit his demands, to see the work of ar tin isolation and to tear it from the wide context to which he knew it belonged. After the most exhausting efforts to bring to expression in it everything which was connected with it in his thoughts, he was forced to abandon it in an unfinished state or to declare that it was incomplete.

1. ['The sun does not move.' *Quaderni d'Anatomia*, 1–6, Royal Library, Windsor, V, 25.]

2. See the enumeration of his scientific achievements in the fine biographical introduction by Marie Herzfeld (1906), in the various essays of the *Conferenze Fiorentine* (1910), and elsewhere.

The artist had once taken the investigator into his service to assist him; now the servant had become the stronger and suppressed his master.

When we find that in the picture presented by a person's character a single instinct has developed an excessive strength, as did the craving for knowledge in Leonardo, we look for the explanation in a special disposition – though about its determinants (which are probably organic) scarcely anything is yet known. Our psycho-analytic studies of neurotic people have however led us to form two further expectations which it would be gratifying to find confirmed in each particular case. We consider it probable that an instinct like this of excessive strength was already active in the subject's earliest childhood, and that its supremacy was established by impressions in the child's life. We make the further assumption that it found reinforcement from what were originally sexual instinctual forces, so that later it could take the place of a part of the subject's sexual life. Thus a person of this sort would, for example, pursue research with the same passionate devotion that another would give to his love, and he would be able to investigate instead of loving. We would venture to infer that it is not only in the example of the instinct to investigate that there has been a sexual reinforcement, but also in most other cases where an instinct is of special intensity.

Observation of men's daily lives shows us that most people succeed in directing very considerable portions of their sexual instinctual forces to their professional activity. The sexual instinct is particularly well fitted to make contributions of this kind since it is endowed with a capacity for sublimation: that is, it has the power to replace its immediate aim by other aims which may be valued more highly and which are not sexual. We accept this process as proved whenever the history of a person's childhood – that is, the history of his mental development – shows that in childhood this over-powerful instinct was in the service of sexual interests. We find further confirmation if a striking atrophy occurs in the sexual life of maturity, as though a portion of sexual activity had now been replaced by the activity of the over-powerful instinct.

There seem to be special difficulties in applying these expectations to the case of an over-powerful instinct for investigation, since precisely in the case of children there is a reluctance to credit them with either this serious instinct or any noteworthy sexual interests. However, these difficulties are easily overcome. The curiosity of small children is manifested in their untiring love of asking questions; this is bewildering to the adult so long as he fails to understand that all these questions are merely circumlocutions and that they cannot come to an end because the child is only trying to make them take the place of a question which he does *not* ask. When he grows bigger and becomes better informed this expression of curiosity often comes to a sudden end. Psycho-analytic investigation provides us with a full explanation by teaching us that many, perhaps most children, or at least the most gifted ones, pass through a period, beginning when they are about three, which may be called the period of *infantile sexual researches*. So far as we know, the curiosity of children of this age does not awaken spontaneously, but is aroused by the impression made by some important event – by the actual birth of a little brother or sister, or by a fear of it based on external experiences – in which the child perceives a threat to his selfish interests. Researches are directed to the question of where babies come from, exactly as if the child were looking for ways and means to avert so undesired an event. In this way we have been astonished to learn that children refuse to believe the bits of information that are given them – for example that they energetically reject the fable of the stork with its wealth of mythological meaning – that they date their intellectual independence from this act of disbelief, and that they often feel in serious opposition to adults and in fact never afterwards forgive them for having deceived them here about the true facts of the case. They investigate along their own lines, divine the baby's presence inside its mother's body, and following the lead of the impulses of their own sexuality, form theories of babies originating from eating, of their being born through the bowels, and of the obscure part played by the father. By that time they already have a notion of the sexual act, which appears to them to be something hostile and violent. But since their own sexual constitution has not yet reached the point of being able to produce babies, their investigation of where babies come from must inevitably come to nothing too and be abandoned as insoluble. The impression caused by this failure in the first attempt at intellectual independence appears to be of a lasting and deeply depressing kind.[1]

When the period of infantile sexual researches has been terminated by a wave of energetic sexual repression, the instinct for research has three distinct possible

1. These improbable-sounding assertions can be confirmed from a study of my 'Analysis of a Phobia in a Five-Year-Old Boy' (1909) and of similar observations. [Before 1924 these last words ran: 'and of the similar observation in Volume II of the *Jahrbuch für psychoanalytische und psychopathologische Forschungen*' – a reference to Jung (1910).] In a paper on 'The Sexual Theories of Children' (1908*b*) I wrote: 'This brooding and doubting, however, becomes the prototype of all later intellectual work directed towards the solution of problems, and the first failure has a crippling effect on the child's whole future.'

vicissitudes open to it owing to its early connexion with sexual interests. In the first of these, research shares the fate of sexuality; thenceforward curiosity remains inhibited and the free activity of intelligence may be limited for the whole of the subject's lifetime, especially as shortly after this the powerful religious inhibition of thought is brought into play by education. This is the type characterized by neurotic inhibition. We know very well that the intellectual weakness which has been acquired in this way gives an effective impetus to the outbreak of a neurotic illness. In a second type the intellectual development is sufficiently strong to resist the sexual repression which has hold of it. Some time after the infantile sexual researches have come to an end, the intelligence, having grown stronger, recalls the old association and offers its help in evading sexual repression, and the suppressed sexual activities of research return from the unconscious in the form of compulsive brooding, naturally in a distorted and unfree form, but sufficiently powerful to sexualize thinking itself and to colour intellectual operations with the pleasure and anxiety that belong to sexual processes proper. Here investigation becomes a sexual activity, often the exclusive one, and the feeling that comes from settling things in one's mind and explaining them replaces sexual satisfaction; but the interminable character of the child's researches is also repeated in the fact that this brooding never ends and that the intellectual feeling, so much desired, of having found a solution recedes more and more into the distance.

In virtue of a special disposition, the third type, which is the rarest and most perfect, escapes both inhibition of thought and neurotic compulsive thinking. It is true that here too sexual repression comes about, but it does not succeed in relegating a component instinct of sexual desire to the unconscious. Instead, the libido evades the fate of repression by being sublimated from the very beginning into curiosity and by becoming attached to the powerful instinct for research as a reinforcement. Here, too, the research becomes to some extent compulsive and a substitute for sexual activity; but owing to the complete difference in the underlying psychical processes (sublimation instead of an irruption from the unconscious) the quality of neurosis is absent; there is no attachment to the original complexes of infantile sexual research, and the instinct can operate freely in the service of intellectual interest. Sexual repression, which has made the instinct so strong through the addition to it of sublimated libido, is still taken into account by the instinct, in that it avoids any concern with sexual themes.

If we reflect on the concurrence in Leonardo of his over-powerful instinct for research and the atrophy of his sexual life (which was restricted to what is called ideal [sublimated] homosexuality) we shall be disposed to claim him as a model instance of our third type. The core of his nature, and the secret of it, would appear to be that after his curiosity had been activated in infancy in the service of sexual interests he succeeded in sublimating the greater part of his libido into an urge for research. But it is not easy, to be sure, to prove that this view is right. To do so we should need some picture of his mental development in the first years of his childhood, and it seems foolish to hope for material of that sort when the accounts of his life are so meagre and so unreliable, and when moreover it is a question of information about circumstances that escape the attention of observers even in relation to people of our own generation.

About Leonardo's youth we know very little. He was

born in 1452 in the little town of Vinci between Florence and Empoli; he was an illegitimate child, which in those days was certainly not considered a grave social stigma; his father was Ser Piero da Vinci, a notary and descended from a family of notaries and farmers who took their name from the locality of Vinci; his mother was a certain Caterina, probably a peasant girl, who later married another native of Vinci. This mother does not occur again in the history of Leonardo's life, and it is only Merezhkovsky – the novelist – who believes that he has succeeded in finding some trace of her. The only definite piece of information about Leonardo's childhood comes in an official document of the year 1457; it is a Florentine land-register for the purpose of taxation, which mentions Leonardo among the members of the household of the Vinci family as the five-year-old illegitimate child of Ser Piero.[1] The marriage of Ser Piero with a certain Donna Albiera remained childless, and it was therefore possible for the young Leonardo to be brought up in his father's house. He did not leave this house till – at what age it is not known – he entered Andrea del Verrocchio's studio as an apprentice. In the year 1472 Leonardo's name was already to be found in the list of members of the *Compagnia dei Pittori*. That is all.

1. Scognamiglio (1900, 15).

TWO

THERE is, so far as I know, only one place in his scientific notebooks where Leonardo inserts a piece of information about his childhood. In a passage about the flight of vultures he suddenly interrupts himself to pursue a memory from very early years which had sprung to his mind:

'It seems that I was always destined to be so deeply concerned with vultures; for I recall as one of my very earliest memories that while I was in my cradle, a vulture came down to me, and opened my mouth with its tail, and struck me many times with its tail against my lips.'[1]

What we have here then is a childhood memory; and certainly one of the strangest sort. It is strange on account of its content and on account of the age to which it is assigned. That a person should be able to retain a memory of his suckling period is perhaps not impossible, but it cannot by any means be regarded as certain. What, however, this memory of Leonardo's asserts – namely that a vulture opened the child's mouth with its tail – sounds so improbable, so fabulous, that

1. '*Questo scriver si distintamente del nibio par che sia mio destino, perchè nella mia prima recordatione della mia infantia e' mi parea che, essendo io in culla, che un nibio venissi a me e mi aprissi la bocca colla sua coda e molte volte mi percuotesse con tal coda dentro alle labbra.*' (*Codex Atlanticus*, F.65 v., as given by Scognamiglio [1900, 22].) [In the German text Freud quotes Herzfeld's translation of the Italian original, and our version above is a rendering of the German. There are in fact two inaccuracies in the German: '*nibio*' should be 'kite' not 'vulture' (see Editor's Note, p. 8), and '*dentro*', 'within', is omitted. This last omission is in fact rectified by Freud himself below (p. 122).]

another view of it, which at a single stroke puts an end to both difficulties, has more to commend it to our judgement. On this view the scene with the vulture would not be a memory of Leonardo's but a phantasy, which he formed at a later date and transposed to his childhood.[1]

This is often the way in which childhood memories originate. Quite unlike conscious memories from the time of maturity, they are not fixed at the moment of being experienced and afterwards repeated, but are only elicited at a later age when childhood is already past; in the process they are altered and falsified, and are put into the service of later trends, so that generally speaking they cannot be sharply distinguished from phantasies. Their nature is perhaps best illustrated by a comparison with the way in which the writing of history

---

1. [*Footnote added* 1919:] In a friendly notice of this book Havelock Ellis (1910) has challenged the view put forward above. He objects that this memory of Leonardo's may very well have had a basis of reality, since children's memories often reach very much further back than is commonly supposed; the large bird in question need not of course have been a vulture. This is a point that I will gladly concede, and as a step towards lessening the difficulty I in turn will offer a suggestion – namely that his mother observed the large bird's visit to her child – an event which may easily have had the significance of an omen in her eyes – and repeatedly told him about it afterwards. As a result, I suggest, he retained the memory of his mother's story, and later, as so often happens, it became possible for him to take it for a memory of an experience of his own. However, this alteration does no damage to the force of my general account. It happens, indeed, as a general rule that the phantasies about their childhood which people construct at a late date are attached to trivial but real events of this early, and normally forgotten, period. There must thus have been some secret reason for bringing into prominence a real event of no importance and for elaborating it in the sort of way Leonardo did in his story of the bird, which he dubbed a vulture, and of its remarkable behaviour.

originated among the peoples of antiquity. As long as a nation was small and weak it gave no thought to the writing of its history. Men tilled the soil of their land, fought for their existence against their neighbours, and tried to gain territory from them and to acquire wealth. It was an age of heroes, not of historians. Then came another age, an age of reflection: men felt themselves to be rich and powerful, and now felt a need to learn where they had come from and how they had developed. Historical writing, which had begun to keep a continuous record of the present, now also cast a glance back to the past, gathered traditions and legends, interpreted the traces of antiquity that survived in customs and usages, and in this way created a history of the past. It was inevitable that this early history should have been an expression of present beliefs and wishes rather than a true picture of the past; for many things had been dropped from the nation's memory, while others were distorted, and some remains of the past were given a wrong interpretation in order to fit in with contemporary ideas. Moreover people's motive for writing history was not objective curiosity but a desire to influence their contemporaries, to encourage and inspire them, or to hold a mirror up before them. A man's conscious memory of the events of his maturity is in every way comparable to the first kind of historical writing [which was a chronicle of current events]; while the memories that he has of his childhood correspond, as far as their origins and reliability are concerned, to the history of a nation's earliest days, which was compiled later and for tendentious reasons.[1]

1. [Chapter 4 of *The Psychopathology of Everyday Life* (1901) deals with childhood memories and screen-memories, and, in an addition made to it in 1907, Freud makes the same comparison with historical writing.]

If, then, Leonardo's story about the vulture that visited him in his cradle is only a phantasy from a later period, one might suppose it could hardly be worth while spending much time on it. One might be satisfied with explaining it on the basis of his inclination, of which he makes no secret, to regard his preoccupation with the flight of birds as pre-ordained by destiny. Yet in underrating this story one would be committing just as great an injustice as if one were carelessly to reject the body of legends, traditions, and interpretations found in a nation's early history. In spite of all the distortions and misunderstandings, they still represent the reality of the past: they are what a people forms out of the experience of its early days and under the dominance of motives that were once powerful and still operate today; and if it were only possible, by a knowledge of all the forces at work, to undo these distortions, there would be no difficulty in disclosing the historical truth lying behind the legendary material. The same holds good for the childhood memories or phantasies of an individual. What someone thinks he remembers from his childhood is not a matter of indifference; as a rule the residual memories – which he himself does not understand – cloak priceless pieces of evidence about the most important features in his mental development.[1]

1. [*Footnote added* 1919:] Since I wrote the above words I have attempted to make similar use of an unintelligible memory dating from the childhood of another man of genius. In the account of his life that Goethe wrote when he was about sixty (*Dichtung und Wahrheit*) there is a description in the first few pages of how, with the encouragement of his neighbours, he slung first some small and then some large pieces of crockery out of the window into the street, so that they were smashed to pieces. This is, indeed, the only scene that he reports from the earliest years of childhood. The sheer inconsequentiality of its content, the way in which it corresponded with the childhood memories of other human beings

As we now possess in the techniques of psycho-analysis excellent methods for helping us to bring this concealed material to light, we may venture to fill in the gap in Leonardo's life story by analysing his childhood phantasy. And if in doing so we remain dissatisfied with the degree of certainty which we achieve, we shall have to console ourselves with the reflection that so many other studies of this great and enigmatic man have met with no better fate.

If we examine with the eyes of a psycho-analyst Leonardo's phantasy of the vulture, it does not appear strange for long. We seem to recall having come across

---

who did not become particularly great, and the absence in this passage of any mention of the young brother who was born when Goethe was three and three-quarters, and who died when he was nearly ten – all this induced me to undertake an analysis of this childhood memory. (This child is in fact mentioned at a later point in the book, where Goethe dwells on the many illnesses of childhood.) I hoped to be able as a result to replace it by something which would be more in keeping with the context of Goethe's account and whose content would make it worthy of preservation and of the place he has given it in the history of his life. The short analysis ['A Childhood Recollection from *Dichtung und Wahrheit*' (1917)] made it possible for the throwing-out of the crockery to be recognized as a magical act directed against a troublesome intruder; and at the place in the book where he describes the episode the intention is to triumph over the fact that a second son was not in the long run permitted to disturb Goethe's close relation with his mother. If the earliest memory of childhood, preserved in disguises such as these, should be concerned – in Goethe's case as well as in Leonardo's – with the mother, what would be so surprising in that? [In the 1919 edition the phrase 'and the absence in this passage of any mention of the young brother . . .' ran '. . . and the remarkable absence of any mention whatever of a young brother . . .' It was given its present form, and the parenthesis that follows it was added, in 1923. The alteration is explained in a footnote added in 1924 to the Goethe paper (1917), *Standard Ed.*, **17**, 151*n*.]

the same sort of thing in many places, for example in dreams; so that we may venture to translate the phantasy from its own special language into words that are generally understood. The translation is then seen to point to an erotic content. A tail, *coda*, is one of the most familiar symbols and substitutive expressions for the male organ, in Italian no less than in other languages;[1] the situation in the phantasy of a vulture opening the child's mouth and beating about inside it[2] vigorously with its tail, corresponds to the idea of an act of fellatio, a sexual act in which the penis is put into the mouth of the person involved. It is strange that this phantasy is so completely passive in character; moreover it resembles certain dreams and phantasies found in women or passive homosexuals (who play the part of the woman in sexual relations).

I hope the reader will restrain himself and not allow a surge of indignation to prevent his following psychoanalysis any further because it leads to an unpardonable aspersion on the memory of a great and pure man the very first time it is applied to his case. Such indignation, it is clear, will never be able to tell us the significance of Leonardo's childhood phantasy; at the same time Leonardo had acknowledged the phantasy in the most unambiguous fashion, and we cannot abandon our

1. [Cf. the 'Original Record' of the case of the 'Rat Man', *Standard Ed.*, **10**, 311. – It may be pointed out (supposing the bird to have been in fact a kite) that the kite's long forked tail is one of its noticeable features and plays a large part in the virtuosity of its movements in the air and no doubt attracted Leonardo's attention in his observations of flight. The symbolic meaning of its *coda*, discussed by Freud in this passage, seems to be confirmed by a remark in an ornithological account of the kite published in *The Times* (7 July 1956): 'At times the tail is fanned out at right angles to its normal plane.']

2. [See end of footnote on p. 117.]

expectation – or, if it sounds better, our prejudice – that a phantasy of this kind must have *some* meaning, in the same way as any other psychical creation: a dream, a vision, or a delirium. Let us rather therefore give a fair hearing for a while to the work of analysis, which indeed has not yet spoken its last word.

The inclination to take a man's sexual organ into the mouth and suck at it, which in respectable society is considered a loathsome sexual perversion, is nevertheless found with great frequency among women of today – and of earlier times as well, as ancient sculptures show – and in the state of being in love it appears completely to lose its repulsive character. Phantasies derived from this inclination are found by doctors even in women who have not become aware of the possibilities of obtaining sexual satisfaction in this way by reading Krafft-Ebing's *Psychopathia Sexualis* or from other sources of information. Women, it seems, find no difficulty in producing this kind of wishful phantasy spontaneously.[1] Further investigation informs us that this situation, which morality condemns with such severity, may be traced to an origin of the most innocent kind. It only repeats in a different form a situation in which we all once felt comfortable – when we were still in our suckling days ('*essendo io in culla*')[2] and took our mother's (or wet-nurse's) nipple into our mouth and sucked at it. The organic impression of this experience – the first source of pleasure in our life – doubtless remains indelibly printed on us; and when at a later date the child becomes familiar with the cow's udder whose function is that of a nipple, but whose shape and position under the belly make it resemble a

1. On this point compare my 'Fragment of an Analysis of a Case of Hysteria' (1905*b*) [*Standard Ed.*, **7**, 51].

2. ['While I was in my cradle.' See footnote 1, p. 117 above.]

penis, the preliminary stage has been reached which will later enable him to form the repellent sexual phantasy.[1]

Now we understand why Leonardo assigned the memory of his supposed experience with the vulture to his suckling period. What the phantasy conceals is merely a reminiscence of sucking – or being suckled – at his mother's breast, a scene of human beauty that he, like so many artists, undertook to depict with his brush, in the guise of the mother of God and her child. There is indeed another point which we do not yet understand and which we must not lose sight of: this reminiscence, which has the same importance for both sexes, has been transformed by the man Leonardo into a passive homosexual phantasy. For the time being we shall put aside the question of what there may be to connect homosexuality with sucking at the mother's breast, merely recalling that tradition does in fact represent Leonardo as a man with homosexual feelings. In this connexion, it is irrelevant to our purpose whether the charge brought against the young Leonardo [pp. 104–5] was justified or not. What decides whether we describe someone as an invert[2] is not his actual behaviour, but his emotional attitude.

Our interest is next claimed by another unintelligible feature of Leonardo's childhood phantasy. We interpret the phantasy as one of being suckled by his mother, and we find his mother replaced by – a vulture. Where does this vulture come from and how does it happen to be found in its present place?

At this point a thought comes to the mind from such a remote quarter that it would be tempting to set it aside. In the hieroglyphics of the ancient Egyptians the

1. [Cf. the analysis of 'Little Hans', *Standard Ed.*, **10**, 7.]
2. [In 1910 only: 'a homosexual'.]

mother is represented by a picture of a vulture.[1] The Egyptians also worshipped a mother goddess, who was represented as having a vulture's head, or else several heads, of which at least one was a vulture's.[2] This goddess's name was pronounced *Mut*. Can the similarity to the sound of our word *Mutter* ['mother'] be merely a coincidence? There is, then, some real connexion between vulture and mother – but what help is that to us? For have we any right to expect Leonardo to know of it, seeing that the first man who succeeded in reading hieroglyphics was François Champollion (1790–1832)?[3]

It would be interesting to inquire how it could be that the ancient Egyptians came to choose the vulture as a symbol of motherhood. Now the religion and civilization of the Egyptians were objects of scientific curiosity even to the Greeks and the Romans: and long before we ourselves were able to read the monuments of Egypt we had at our disposal certain pieces of information about them derived from the extant writings of classical antiquity. Some of these writings were by well-known authors, such as Strago, Plutarch, and Ammianus Marcellinus; while others bear unfamiliar names and are uncertain in their source of origin and their date of composition, like the *Hieroglyphica* of Horapollo Nilous and the book of oriental priestly wisdom which has come down to us under the name of the god Hermes Trismegistos. We learn from these sources that the vulture was regarded as a symbol of motherhood because only female vultures were believed to exist; there were, it was thought, no males of this

1. Horapollo (*Hieroglyphica* i, 11): 'Μητέρα δὲ γράφοντες . . . γῦπα ζωγραφοῦσιν.' ['To denote a mother . . . they delineate a vulture.']

2. Roscher (1894–97), Lanzone (1882).

3. Hartleben (1906).

species.[1] A counterpart to this restriction to one sex was also known to the natural history of antiquity: in the case of the scarabaeus beetle, which the Egyptians worshipped as divine, it was thought that only males existed.[2]

How then were vultures supposed to be impregnated if all of them were female? This is a point fully explained in a passage in Horapollo.[3] At a certain time these birds pause in mid flight, open their vagina, and are impregnated by the wind.

We have now unexpectedly reached a position where we can take something as very probable which only a short time before we had to reject as absurd. It is quite possible that Leonardo was familiar with the scientific fable which was responsible for the vulture being used by the Egyptians as a pictorial representation of the idea of mother. He was a wide reader and his interest embraced all branches of literature and learning. In the *Codex Atlanticus* we find a catalogue of all the books he

---

1. 'γῦπα δὲ ἄρρενα οὔ φασι γινέσθαι ποτε, ἀλλὰ θηλείας ἁπάσας.' ['They say that no male vulture has ever existed but all are females.' Aelian, *De Natura Animalium*, II, 46.] Quoted by von Römer (1903, 732).

2. Plutarch: '*Veluti scarabaeos mares tantum esse putarunt Aegyptii sic inter vultures mares non inveniri statuerunt.*' ['Just as they believed that only male scarabs existed, so the Egyptians concluded that no male vultures were to be found.' Freud has here inadvertently attributed to Plutarch a sentence which is in fact a gloss by Leemans (1835, 171) on Horapollo.]

3. *Horapollinis Niloi Hieroglyphica*, ed. Leemans (1835, 14). The words that refer to the vulture's sex run: 'μητέρα μέν, ἐπειδὴ ἄρρεν ἐν τούτῳ τῷ γένει τῶν ζῴων οὐχ ὑπάρχει.' ['(They use the picture of a vulture to denote) a mother, because in this race of creatures there are no males.' – It seems as though the wrong passage from Horapollo is quoted here. The phrase in the text implies that what we should have here is the myth of the vulture's impregnation by the wind.]

possessed at a particular date,[1] and in addition numerous jottings on other books that he had borrowed from
friends; and if we may judge by the extracts from his
notes by Richter [1883],[2] the extent of his reading can
hardly be overestimated. Early works on natural history
were well represented among them in addition to contemporary books; and all of them were already in print
at the time. Milan was in fact the leading city in Italy
for the new art of printing.

On proceeding further we come across a piece of
information which can turn the probability that Leonardo knew the fable of the vulture into a certainty. The
learned editor and commentator on Horapollo has the
following note on the text already quoted above
[Leemans (1835, 172)]: '*Caeterum hanc fabulam de vulturibus
cupide amplexi sunt Patres Ecclesiastici, ut ita argumento ex
rerum natura petito refutarent eos, qui Virginis partum nega-
bant; itaque apud omnes fere hujus rei mentio occurrit.*'[3]

So the fable of the single sex of vultures and their
mode of conception remained something very far from
an unimportant anecdote like the analogous tale of the
scarabaeus beetle; it had been seized on by the Fathers
of the Church so that they could have at their disposal
a proof drawn from natural history to confront those
who doubted sacred history. If vultures were described
in the best accounts of antiquity as depending on the
wind for impregnation, why could not the same thing
have also happened on one occasion with a human
female? Since the fable of the vulture could be turned

1. Müntz (1899, 282).   2. Müntz (ibid.).

3. ['But this story about the vulture was eagerly taken up
by the Fathers of the Church, in order to refute, by means of a
proof drawn from the natural order, those who denied the Virgin Birth. The subject is therefore mentioned in almost all of
them.']

to this account 'almost all' the Fathers of the Church made a practice of telling it, and thus it can hardly be doubted that Leonardo too came to know of it through its being favoured by so wide a patronage.

We can now reconstruct the origin of Leonardo's vulture phantasy. He once happened to read in one of the Fathers or in a book on natural history the statement that all vultures were females and could reproduce their kind without any assistance from a male: and at that point a memory sprang to his mind, which was transformed into the phantasy we have been discussing, but which meant to signify that he also had been such a vulture-child – he had had a mother, but no father. With this memory was associated, in the only way in which impressions of so great an age can find expression, an echo of the pleasure he had had at his mother's breast. The allusion made by the Fathers of the Church to the idea of the Blessed Virgin and her child – an idea cherished by every artist – must have played its part in helping the phantasy to appear valuable and important to him. Indeed in this way he was able to identify himself with the child Christ, the comforter and saviour not of this one woman alone.

Our aim in dissecting a childhood phantasy is to separate the real memory that it contains from the later motives that modify and distort it. In Leonardo's case we believe that we now know the real content of the phantasy: the replacement of his mother by the vulture indicates that the child was aware of his father's absence and found himself alone with his mother. The fact of Leonardo's illegitimate birth is in harmony with his vulture phantasy; it was only on this account that he could compare himself to a vulture child. But the next reliable fact that we possess about his youth is that by the time he was five he had been received into his father's household. We are completely ignorant when that happened – whether it was a few months after his birth or whether it was a few weeks before the drawing-up of the land-register [p. 116]. It is here that the interpretation of the vulture phantasy comes in: Leonardo, it seems to tell us, spent the critical first years of his life not by the side of his father and stepmother, but with his poor, forsaken, real mother, so that he had time to feel the absence of his father. This seems a slender and yet a somewhat daring conclusion to have emerged from our psycho-analytic efforts, but its significance will increase as we continue our investigation. Its certainty is reinforced when we consider the circumstances that did in fact operate in Leonardo's childhood. In the same year that Leonardo was born, the sources tell us, his father, Ser Piero da Vinci, married Donna Albiera, a lady of good birth; it was to the childlessness of this marriage that the boy owed his reception into his father's (or rather his grandfather's) house – an event which had taken place by the time he was five years old, as the document attests. Now it is not usual at the start of a marriage to put an illegitimate offspring into the care of the young bride who still expects to be blessed with children of her own. Years of disappointment must surely first have elapsed before it was decided to adopt the illegitimate child – who had probably grown up an attractive young boy – as a compensation for the absence of the legitimate children that had been hoped for. It fits in best with the interpretation of the vulture phantasy if at least three years of Leonardo's life, and perhaps five, had elapsed before he could exchange the solitary person of his mother for a parental couple. And by then it was too late. In the first three or four years of life certain impressions become fixed and ways of reacting to the outside world are established which can never be deprived of their importance by later experiences.

If it is true that the unintelligible memories of a person's childhood and the phantasies that are built on them invariably emphasize the most important elements in his mental development, then it follows that the fact which the vulture phantasy confirms, namely that Leonardo spent the first years of his life alone with his mother, will have been of decisive influence in the formation of his inner life. An inevitable effect of this state of affairs was that the child – who was confronted in his early life with one problem more than other children – began to brood on this riddle with special intensity, and so at a tender age became a researcher, tormented as he was by the great question of where babies come from and what the father has to do with their origin.[1] It was a vague suspicion that his researches and the history of his childhood were connected in this way which later prompted him to exclaim that he had been destined from the first to investigate the problem of the flight of birds since he had been visited by a vulture as he lay in his cradle. Later on it will not be difficult to show how his curiosity about the flight of birds was derived from the sexual researches of his childhood.

1. [Cf. 'The Sexual Theories of Children' (1908*b*).]

THREE

In Leonardo's childhood phantasy we have taken the element of the vulture to represent the real content of his memory, while the context in which Leonardo himself placed his phantasy has thrown a bright light on the importance which that content had for his later life. In proceeding with our work of interpretation we now come up against the strange problem of why this content has been recast into a homosexual situation. The mother who suckles her child – or to put it better, at whose breast the child sucks – has been turned into a vulture that puts its tail into the child's mouth. We have asserted [p. 122] that, according to the usual way in which language makes use of substitutes, the vulture's *coda* cannot possibly signify anything other than a male genital, a penis. But we do not understand how imaginative activity can have succeeded in endowing precisely this bird which is a mother with the distinguishing mark of masculinity; and in view of this absurdity we are at a loss how to reduce this creation of Leonardo's phantasy to any rational meaning.

However, we should not despair, as we reflect on the number of apparently absurd dreams that we have in the past compelled to give up their meaning. Is there any reason why a memory of childhood should offer us more difficulty than a dream?

Remembering that it is unsatisfactory when a peculiar feature is found singly, let us hasten to add another to it which is even more striking.[1]

The vulture-headed Egyptian goddess Mut, a figure

1. [Cf. some similar remarks by Freud in *The Interpretation of Dreams* (1900), *Standard Ed.*, **4**, 135–6.]

without any personal character according to Drexler's article in Roscher's lexicon, was often merged with other mother goddesses of a more strongly marked individuality, like Isis and Hathor, but at the same time she maintained her separate existence and cult. A special feature of the Egyptian pantheon was that the individual gods did not disappear in the process of syncretization. Alongside the fusion of gods the individual divinities continued to exist in independence. Now this vulture-headed mother goddess was usually represented by the Egyptians with a phallus;[1] her body was female, as the breasts indicated, but it also had a male organ in a state of erection.

In the goddess Mut, then, we find the same combination of maternal and masculine characteristics as in Leonardo's phantasy of the vulture. Are we to explain this coincidence by assuming that from studying his books [cf. pp. 126-7] Leonardo had also learnt of the androgynous nature of the maternal vulture? Such a possibility is more than questionable; it appears that the sources to which he had access contained no information about this remarkable feature. It is more plausible to trace the correspondence back to a common factor operative in both cases but still unknown.

Mythology can teach us that an androgynous structure, a combination of male and female sex characters, was an attribute not only of Mut but also of other deities like Isis and Hathor – though perhaps of these only in so far as they too had a maternal nature and became amalgamated with Mut (Römer, 1903). It teaches us further that other Egyptian deities, like Neith of Sais – from whom the Greek Athene was later derived – were

1. See the illustrations in Lanzone (1882, Plates CXXXVI-CXXXVIII).

originally conceived of as androgynous, i.e. as herma-phrodite, and that the same was true of many of the *Greek* gods, especially of those associated with Dionysus, but also of Aphrodite, who was later restricted to the role of a female goddess of love. Mythology may then offer the explanation that the addition of a phallus to the female body is intended to denote the primal crea-tive force of nature, and that all these hermaphrodite divinities are expressions of the idea that only a com-bination of male and female elements can give a worthy representation of divine perfection. But none of these considerations gives us an explanation of the puzzling psychological fact that the human imagination does not boggle at endowing a figure which is intended to em-body the essence of the mother with the mark of male potency which is the opposite of everything maternal.

Infantile sexual theories provide the explanation. There was once a time when the male genital was found compatible with the picture of the mother.[1] When a male child first turns his curiosity to the riddles of sexual life, he is dominated by his interest in his own genital. He finds that part of his body too valuable and too important for him to be able to believe that it could be missing in other people whom he feels he resembles so much. As he cannot guess that there exists another type of genital structure of equal worth, he is forced to make the assumption that all human beings, women as well as men, possess a penis like his own. This preconception is so firmly planted in the youthful investigator that it is not destroyed even when he first observes the genitals of little girls. His perception tells him, it is true, that there is something different from what there is in him, but he is incapable of admitting to himself that the content of this perception is that he cannot find a penis

1. [Cf. 'The Sexual Theories of Children' (1908*b*).]

in girls. That the penis could be missing strikes him as an uncanny and intolerable idea, and so in an attempt at a compromise, he comes to the conclusion that little girls have a penis as well, only it is still very small; it will grow later.[1] If it seems from later observations that this expectation is not realized, he has another remedy at his disposal: little girls too had a penis, but it was cut off and in its place was left a wound. This theoretical advance already makes use of personal experiences of a distressing kind: the boy in the meantime has heard the threat that the organ which is so dear to him will be taken away from him if he shows his interest in it too plainly. Under the influence of this threat of castration he now sees the notion he has gained of the female genitals in a new light; henceforth he will tremble for his masculinity, but at the same time he will despise the unhappy creatures on whom the cruel punishment has, as he supposes, already fallen.[2]

Before the child comes under the dominance of the castration-complex – at a time when he still holds women at full value – he begins to display an intense

1. Compare the observations in the *Jahrbuch für psychoanalytische und psychopathologische Forschungen* [i.e. Freud, 1909, 'Little Hans', *Standard Ed.*, **10**, 11, and Jung, 1910. – *Added* 1919:], in the *Internationale Zeitschrift für ärztliche Psychoanalyse* and in [the section dealing with children in] *Imago*.

2. [*Footnote added* 1919:] The conclusion strikes me as inescapable that here we may also trace one of the roots of the anti-semitism which appears with such elemental force and finds such irrational expression among the nations of the West. Circumcision is unconsciously equated with castration. If we venture to carry our conjectures back to the primeval days of the human race we can surmise that originally circumcision must have been a milder substitute, designed to take the place of castration. [Further discussion on this will be found in a footnote to the analysis of 'Little Hans' (1909), *Standard Ed.*, **10**, 36, and in *Moses and Monotheism* (1939), Chapter III, Part I, Section D.]

desire to look, as an erotic instinctual activity. He wants
to see other people's genitals, at first in all probability
to compare them with his own. The erotic attraction
that comes from his mother soon culminates in a longing
for her genital organ, which he takes to be a penis.
With the discovery, which is not made till later, that
women do not have a penis, this longing often turns
into its opposite and gives place to a feeling of disgust
which in the years of puberty can become the cause of
psychical impotence, misogyny, and permanent homosexuality. But the fixation on the object that was once
strongly desired, the woman's penis, leaves indelible
traces on the mental life of the child, who has pursued
that portion of his infantile sexual researches with particular thoroughness. Fetishistic reverence for a woman's foot and shoe appears to take the foot merely as a
substitutive symbol for the woman's penis which was
once revered and later missed; without knowing it,
coupeurs de nattes[1] play the part of people who carry
out an act of castration on the female genital organ.

People will not reach a proper understanding of the
activities of children's sexuality and will probably take
refuge in declaring that what has been said here is
incredible, so long as they cling to the attitude taken
up by our civilization of depreciating the genitals and
the sexual functions. To understand the mental life of
children we require analogies from primitive times.
Through a long series of generations the genitals have
been for us the *pudenda*, objects of shame, and even
(as a result of further successful sexual repression) of
disgust. If one makes a broad survey of the sexual life
of our time and in particular of the classes who sustain
human civilization, one is tempted to declare that[2] it is

1. [Perverts who enjoy cutting off females' hair.]
2. [The sentence up to this point was added in 1919.]

only with reluctance that the majority of those alive today obey the command to propagate their kind; they feel that their dignity as human beings suffers and is degraded in the process. What is to be found among us in the way of another view of sexual life is confined to the uncultivated lower strata of society; among the higher and more refined classes it is concealed, since it is considered culturally inferior, and it ventures to put itself into practice only in the face of a bad conscience. In the primeval days of the human race it was a different story. The laborious compilations of the student of civilization provide convincing evidence that originally the genitals were the pride and hope of living beings; they were worshipped as gods and transmitted the divine nature of their functions to all newly learned human activities. As a result of the sublimation of their basic nature there arose innumerable divinities; and at the time when the connexion between official religions and sexual activity was already hidden from the general consciousness, secret cults devoted themselves to keeping it alive among a number of initiates. In the course of cultural development so much of the divine and sacred was ultimately extracted from sexuality that the exhausted remnant fell into contempt. But in view of the indelibility that is characteristic of all mental traces, it is surely not surprising that even the most primitive forms of genital-worship can be shown to have existed in very recent times and that the language, customs, and superstitions of mankind today contain survivals from every phase of this process of development.[1]

Impressive analogies from biology have prepared us to find that the individual's mental development repeats the course of human development in an abbreviated form; and the conclusions which psycho-analytic

1. Cf. Knight [1768].

research into the child's mind has reached concerning the high value set on the genitals in infancy will not therefore strike us as improbable. The child's assumption that his mother has a penis is thus the common source from which are derived the androgynously-formed mother goddesses such as the Egyptian Mut and the vulture's *coda* in Leonardo's childhood phantasy. It is in fact only due to a misunderstanding that we describe these representations of gods as hermaphrodite in the medical sense of the word. In none of them is there a combination of the true genitals of both sexes – a combination which, to the abhorrence of all beholders, is found in some cases of malformation; all that has happened is that the male organ has been added to the breasts which are the mark of a mother, just as it was present in the child's first idea of his mother's body. This form of the mother's body, the revered creation of primeval phantasy, has been preserved for the faithful by mythology. We can now provide the following translation of the emphasis given to the vulture's tail in Leonardo's phantasy: 'That was a time when my fond curiosity was directed to my mother, and when I still believed she had a genital organ like my own.' Here is more evidence of Leonardo's early sexual researches, which in our opinion had a decisive effect on the whole of his later life.

At this point a little reflection will remind us that we ought not to feel satisfied yet with the way the vulture's tail in Leonardo's childhood phantasy has been explained. Something more seems to be contained in it which we do not yet understand. Its most striking feature, after all, was that it changed sucking at the mother's breast into being suckled, that is, into passivity, and thus into a situation whose nature is undoubtedly homosexual. When we remember the historical probability of Leonardo having behaved in his life as one who was emotionally homosexual, the question is forced upon us whether this phantasy does not indicate the existence of a causal connexion between Leonardo's relation with his mother in childhood and his later manifest, if ideal [sublimated], homosexuality. We should not venture to infer a connexion of this sort from Leonardo's distorted reminiscence if we did not know from the psycho-analytic study of homosexual patients that such a connexion does exist and is in fact an intimate and necessary one.

Homosexual men, who have in our times taken vigorous action against the restrictions imposed by law on their sexual activity, are fond of representing themselves, through their theoretical spokesmen, as being from the outset a distinct sexual species, as an intermediate sexual stage, as a 'third sex'. They are, they claim, men who are innately compelled by organic determinants to find pleasure in men and have been debarred from obtaining it in women. Much as one would be glad on grounds of humanity to endorse their claims, one must treat their theories with some reserve, for they have been advanced without regard for the psychical genesis of homosexuality. Psycho-analysis offers the means of filling this gap and of putting the assertions of homosexuals to the test. It has succeeded in the task only in the case of a small number of persons, but all the investigations undertaken so far have yielded the same surprising result.[1] In all our male homosexual cases the subjects had had a very intense erotic attachment to a female person, as a rule their mother, during

1. I refer in particular to the investigations of I. Sadger, which I can in the main confirm from my own experience. I am also aware that Wilhelm Stekel of Vienna and Sándor Ferenczi of Budapest have arrived at the same results.

the first period of childhood, which is afterwards forgotten; this attachment was evoked or encouraged by too much tenderness on the part of the mother herself, and further reinforced by the small part played by the father during their childhood. Sadger emphasizes the fact that the mothers of his homosexual patients were frequently masculine women, women with energetic traits of character, who were able to push the father out of his proper place. I have occasionally seen the same thing, but I was more strongly impressed by cases in which the father was absent from the beginning or left the scene at an early date, so that the boy found himself left entirely under feminine influence. Indeed it almost seems as though the presence of a strong father would ensure that the son made the correct decision in his choice of object, namely someone of the opposite sex.[1]

After this preliminary stage a transformation sets in whose mechanism is known to us but whose motive forces we do not yet understand. The child's love for

1. [*Footnote added* 1919:] Psycho-analytic research has contributed two facts that are beyond question to the understanding of homosexuality, without at the same time supposing that it has exhausted the causes of this sexual aberration. The first is the fixation of the erotic needs on the mother which has been mentioned above; the other is contained in the statement that everyone, even the most normal person, is capable of making a homosexual object-choice, and has done so at some time in his life, and either still adheres to it in his unconscious or else protects himself against it by vigorous counter-attitudes. These two discoveries put an end both to the claim of homosexuals to be regarded as a 'third sex' and to what has been believed to be the important distinction between innate and acquired homosexuality. The presence of somatic characters of the other sex (the quota provided by physical hermaphroditism) is highly conducive to the homosexual object-choice becoming manifest; but it is not decisive. It must be stated with regret that those who speak for the homosexuals in the field of science have been incapable of learning anything from the established findings of psycho-analysis.

his mother cannot continue to develop consciously any further; it succumbs to repression. The boy represses his love for his mother: he puts himself in her place, identifies himself with her, and takes his own person as a model in whose likeness he chooses the new objects of his love. In this way he has become a homosexual. What he has in fact done is to slip back to auto-erotism: for the boys whom he now loves as he grows up are after all only substitutive figures and revivals of himself in childhood – boys whom he loves in the way in which his mother loved *him* when he was a child. He finds the objects of his love along the path of *narcissism*, as we say; for Narcissus, according to the Greek legend, was a youth who preferred his own reflection to everything else and who was changed into the lovely flower of that name.[1]

Psychological considerations of a deeper kind justify the assertion that a man who has become a homosexual in this way remains unconsciously fixated to the mnemic image of his mother. By repressing his love for his mother he preserves it in his unconscious and from now on remains faithful to her. While he seems to pursue boys and to be their lover, he is in reality running away from the other women who might cause him to be unfaithful. In individual cases direct observation has also enabled us to show that the man who gives the appearance of being susceptible only to the charms of men is in fact attracted by women in the same way as a normal man; but on each occasion he hastens to transfer the excitation he has received from women on to a male

1. [Freud's first published reference to narcissism had appeared only a few months before, in a footnote added to the second edition of his *Three Essays* (1905*a*), *Standard Ed.*, **7**, 145*n*., which was published early in 1910. He had mentioned the concept at a meeting of the Vienna Psycho-Analytical Society on 10 November 1909. For a full-length discussion of the subject see 'On Narcissism: an Introduction' (1914).]

object, and in this manner he repeats over and over again the mechanism by which he acquired his homosexuality.

We are far from wishing to exaggerate the importance of these explanations of the psychical genesis of homosexuality. It is quite obvious that they are in sharp contrast to the official theories of those who speak for homosexuals, but we know that they are not sufficiently comprehensive to make a conclusive explanation of the problem possible. What is for practical reasons called homosexuality may arise from a whole variety of psychosexual inhibitory processes; the particular process we have singled out is perhaps only one among many, and is perhaps related to only one type of 'homosexuality'. We must also admit that the number of cases of our homosexual type in which it is possible to point to the determinants which we require far exceeds the number of those where the deduced effect actually takes place; so that we too cannot reject the part played by unknown constitutional factors, to which the whole of homosexuality is usually traced. We should not have had any cause at all for entering into the psychical genesis of the form of homosexuality we have studied if there were not a strong presumption that Leonardo, whose phantasy of the vulture was our starting-point, was himself a homosexual of this very type.[1]

Few details are known about the sexual behaviour of the great artist and scientist, but we may place confidence in the probability that the assertions of his con-

1. [A more general discussion of homosexuality and its genesis will be found in the first of Freud's *Three Essays* (1905*a*), particularly in a long footnote added between 1910 and 1920, *Standard Ed.*, **7**, 144–7. Among other, later discussions of the subject may be mentioned his case history of a female homosexual (1920*a*) and 'Some Neurotic Mechanisms in Jealousy, Paranoia and Homosexuality' (1922).]

temporaries were not grossly erroneous. In the light of these traditions, then, he appears as a man whose sexual need and activity were exceptionally reduced, as if a higher aspiration had raised him above the common animal need of mankind. It may remain open to doubt whether he ever sought direct sexual satisfaction – and if so, in what manner – or whether he was able to dispense with it altogether. We are however justified in looking into him too for the emotional currents which drive other men imperatively on to perform the sexual act; for we cannot imagine the mental life of any human being in the formation of which sexual desire in the broadest sense – libido – did not have its share, even if that desire has departed far from its original aim, or has refrained from putting itself into effect.

We cannot expect to find in Leonardo anything more than *traces* of untransformed sexual inclination. But these point in one direction and moreover allow him to be reckoned as a homosexual. It has always been emphasized that he took only strikingly handsome boys and youths as pupils. He treated them with kindness and consideration, looked after them, and when they were ill nursed them himself, just as a mother nurses her children and just as his own mother might have tended him. As he had chosen them for their beauty and not for their talent, none of them – Cesare da Sesto, Boltraffio, Andrea Salaino, Francesco Melzi, and others – became a painter of importance. Generally they were unable to make themselves independent of their master, and after his death they disappeared without leaving left any definite mark on the history of art. The others, whose works entitled them to be called his pupils, like Luini and Bazzi, called Sodoma, he probably did not know personally.

We realize that we shall have to meet the objection

that Leonardo's behaviour towards his pupils has nothing at all to do with sexual motives and that it allows no conclusions to be drawn about his particular sexual inclination. Against this we wish to submit with all caution that our view explains some peculiar features of the artist's behaviour which would otherwise have to remain a mystery. Leonardo kept a diary; he made entries in his small hand (written from right to left) which were meant only for himself. It is noteworthy that in this diary he addressed himself in the second person. 'Learn the multiplication of roots from Master Luca.' (Solmi, 1908, 152). 'Get Master d'Abacco to show you how to square the circle.' (Loc. cit.) Or on the occasion of a journey: 'I am going to Milan on business to do with my garden . . . Have two baggage trunks made. Get Boltraffio to show you the turning-lathe and get him to polish a stone on it. Leave the book for Master Andrea il Todesco.' (Ibid., 203).[1] Or a resolution of very different importance: 'You have to show in your treatise that the earth is a star, like the moon or something like it, and thus prove the nobility of our world.' (Herzfeld, 1906, 141.)

In this diary, which, by the way, like the diaries of other mortals, often dismisses the most important events of the day in a few words or else passes them over in complete silence, there are some entries which on account of their strangeness are quoted by all Leonardo's biographers. They are notes of small sums of money spent by the artist – notes recorded with a minute exactness, as if they were made by a pedantically strict and parsimonious head of a household. There is on the

1. Leonardo is behaving here like someone whose habit it was to make his daily confession to another person and who uses his diary as a substitute for him. For a conjecture as to who this person may have been, see Merezhkovsky (1903, 367).

other hand no record of the expenditure of larger sums or any other evidence that the artist was at home in keeping accounts. One of these notes has to do with a new cloak which he bought for his pupil Andrea Salaino:[1]

Silver brocade	15 lire	4	soldi
Crimson velvet for trimming	9 ,,	–	,,
Braid	– ,,	9	,,
Buttons	– ,,	12	,,

Another very detailed note brings together all the expenses he incurred through the bad character and thievish habits of another pupil:[2] 'On the twenty-first day of April, 1490, I began this book and made a new start on the horse.[3] Jacomo came to me on St Mary Magdalen's day, 1490: he is ten years old.' (Marginal note: 'thievish, untruthful, selfish, greedy.') 'On the second day I had two shirts cut out for him, a pair of trousers and a jacket, and when I put the money aside to pay for these things, he stole the money from my purse, and it was never possible to make him own up, although I was absolutely sure of it.' (Marginal note: '4 lire. . . .') The report of the child's misdeeds runs on in this way and ends with the reckoning of expenses: 'In the first year, a cloak, 2 lire; 6 shirts, 4 lire; 3 jackets, 6 lire; 4 pairs of stockings, 7 lire; etc.'[4]

Nothing is further from the wishes of Leonardo's biographers than to try to solve the problems in their hero's mental life by starting from his small weaknesses and peculiarities; and the usual comment that they

1. The text is that given by Merezhkovsky (1903, 282).
2. Or model.
3. For the equestrian statue of Francesco Sforza.
4. The full text is to be found in Herzfeld (1906, 45).

make on these singular accounts is one which lays stress on the artist's kindness and consideration for his pupils. They forget that what calls for explanation is not Leonardo's behaviour, but the fact that he left these pieces of evidence of it behind him. As it is impossible to believe that his motive was that of letting proofs of his good nature fall into our hands, we must assume that it was another motive, an affective one, which led him to write these notes down. What motive it was is not easy to guess, and we should be unable to suggest one if there were not another account found among Leonardo's papers which throws a vivid light on these strangely trifling notes about his pupils' clothing, etc.:

Expenses after Caterina's death for her funeral	27	florins
2 pounds of wax	18	,,
For transporting and erecting the cross	12	,,
Catafalque	4	,,
Pall-bearers	8	,,
For 4 priests and 4 clerks	20	,,
Bell-ringing	2	,,
For the grave-diggers	16	,,
For the licence – to the officials	1	,,
Total	108	florins

Previous expenses:

For the doctor	4	florins
For sugar and candles	12	,,
	16	florins
Grand total	124	florins.[1]

1. Merezhkovsky (1903, 372). As a melancholy example of the uncertainty that surrounds the information, which is in any case scanty enough, about Leonardo's private life, I may mention the fact that the same account is quoted by Solmi (1908, 104) with considerable variations. The most serious one is that soldi are

The novelist Merezhkovsky alone is able to tell us who this Caterina was. From two other short notes[1] he concludes that Leonardo's mother, the poor peasant woman of Vinci, came to Milan in 1493 to visit her son, who was then forty-one; that she fell ill there, was taken to hospital by Leonardo, and when she died was honoured by him with this costly funeral.

This interpretation by the psychological novelist cannot be put to the proof, but it can claim so much inner probability, and is so much in harmony with all that we otherwise know of Leonardo's emotional activity, that I cannot refrain from accepting it as correct. He had succeeded in subjecting his feelings to the yoke of research and in inhibiting their free utterance; but even for him there were occasions when what had been suppressed obtained expression forcibly. The death of the mother he had once loved so dearly was one of these. What we have before us in the account of the costs of the funeral is the expression – distorted out of all recognition – of his mourning for his mother. We wonder how such distortion could come about, and

---

given instead of florins. It may be assumed that florins in this account do not mean the old 'gold florins' but the monetary units which were used later and were worth $1\frac{2}{3}$ lire or $33\frac{1}{3}$ soldi. Solmi makes Caterina a servant who had looked after Leonardo's household for some time. The source from which the two versions of these accounts were taken was not accessible to me. [The figures given actually vary to some extent in the different editions of Freud's own book. The cost of the catafalque is given in 1910 as '12', in 1919 and 1923 as '19', and from 1925 as '4'. Before 1925 the cost of transporting and erecting the cross was given as '4'. For a recent version of the whole text, in Italian and English, see J. P. Richter (1939, **2**, 379).]

1. 'Caterina arrived on 16 July 1493.' – 'Giovannina – a fabulous face – Call on Caterina in the hospital and make inquiries.'

indeed we cannot understand it if we treat it as a normal mental process. But similar processes are well known to us in the abnormal conditions of neurosis and especially of what is known as 'obsessional neurosis'. There we can see how the expression of intense feelings, which have however become unconscious through repression, is displaced on to trivial and even foolish actions. The expression of these repressed feelings has been lowered by the forces opposed to them to such a degree that one would have had to form a most insignificant estimate of their intensity; but the imperative compulsiveness with which this trivial expressive act is performed betrays the real force of the impulses – a force which is rooted in the unconscious and which consciousness would like to deny. Only a comparison such as this with what happens in obsessional neurosis can explain Leonardo's account of the expenses of his mother's funeral. In his unconscious he was still tied to her by erotically coloured feelings, as he had been in childhood. The opposition that came from the subsequent repression of this childhood love did not allow him to set up a different and worthier memorial to her in his diary. But what emerged as a compromise from this neurotic conflict had to be carried out; and thus it was that the account was entered in the diary, and has come to the knowledge of posterity as something unintelligible.

It does not seem a very extravagant step to apply what we have learnt from the funeral account to the reckonings of the pupils' expenses. They would then be another instance of the scanty remnants of Leonardo's libidinal impulses finding expression in a compulsive manner and in a distorted form. On that view, his mother and his pupils, the likenesses of his own boyish beauty, had been his sexual objects – so far as the sexual

147

repression which dominated his nature allows us so to describe them – and the compulsion to note in laborious detail the sums he spent on them betrayed in this strange way his rudimentary conflicts. From this it would appear that Leonardo's erotic life did really belong to the type of homosexuality whose psychical development we have succeeded in disclosing, and the emergence of the homosexual situation in his phantasy of the vulture would become intelligible to us: for its meaning was exactly what we have already asserted of that type. We should have to translate it thus: 'It was through this erotic relation with my mother that I became a homosexual.'[1]

1. The forms of expression in which Leonardo's repressed libido was allowed to show itself – circumstantiality and concern over money – are among the traits of character which result from anal erotism. See my 'Character and Anal Erotism' (1908a).

FOUR

WE have not yet done with Leonardo's vulture phantasy. In words which only too plainly recall a description of a sexual act ('and struck me many times with its tail against[1] my lips'), Leonardo stresses the intensity of the erotic relations between mother and child. From this linking of his mother's (the vulture's) activity with the prominence of the mouth zone it is not difficult to guess that a second memory is contained in the phantasy. This may be translated: 'My mother pressed innumerable passionate kisses on my mouth.' The phantasy is compounded from the memory of being suckled and being kissed by his mother.

Kindly nature has given the artist the ability to express his most secret mental impulses, which are hidden even from himself, by means of the works that he creates; and these works have a powerful effect on others who are strangers to the artist, and who are themselves unaware of the source of their emotion. Can it be that there is nothing in Leonardo's life work to bear witness to what his memory preserved as the strongest impression of his childhood? One would certainly expect there to be something. Yet if one considers the profound transformations through which an impression in an artist's life has to pass before it is allowed to make its contribution to a work of art, one will be bound to keep any claim to certainty in one's demonstration within very modest limits; and this is especially so in Leonardo's case.

Anyone who thinks of Leonardo's paintings will be reminded of a remarkable smile, at once fascinating and

1. [See footnote 1, p. 117.]

149

puzzling, which he conjured up on the lips of his female subjects. It is an unchanging smile, on long, curved lips; it has become a mark of his style and the name 'Leonardesque' has been chosen for it.[1] In the strangely beautiful face of the Florentine Mona Lisa del Giocondo it has produced the most powerful and confusing effect on whoever looks at it. This smile has called for an interpretation, and it has met with many of the most varied kinds, none of which has been satisfactory. *'Voilà quatre siècles bientôt que Monna Lisa fait perdre la tête à tous ceux qui parlent d'elle, après l'avoir longtemps regardée.'*[2]

Muther (1909, **1**, 314) writes: 'What especially casts a spell on the spectator is the daemonic magic of this smile. Hundreds of poets and authors have written about this woman who now appears to smile on us so seductively, and now to stare coldly and without soul into space; and no one has solved the riddle of her smile, no one has read the meaning of her thoughts. Everything, even the landscape, is mysteriously dream-like, and seems to be trembling in a kind of sultry sensuality.'

The idea that two distinct elements are combined in Mona Lisa's smile is one that has struck several critics. They accordingly find in the beautiful Florentine's expression the most perfect representation of the

1. [*Footnote added* 1919:] The connoisseur of art will think here of the peculiar fixed smile found in archaic Greek sculptures – in those, for example, from Aegina; he will perhaps also discover something similar in the figures of Leonardo's teacher Verrocchio and therefore have some misgivings in accepting the arguments that follow.

2. ['For almost four centuries now Mona Lisa has caused all who talk of her, after having gazed on her for long, to lose their heads.'] The words are Gruyer's, quoted by von Seidlitz (1909, **2**, 280).

contrasts which dominate the erotic life of women; the contrast between reserve and seduction, and between the most devoted tenderness and a sensuality that is ruthlessly demanding – consuming men as if they were alien beings. This is the view of Müntz (1899, 417): '*On sait quelle énigme indéchiffrable et passionnante Monna Lisa Gioconda ne cesse depuis bientôt quatre siècles de proposer aux admirateurs pressés devant elle. Jamais artiste(j'emprunte la plume du délicat écrivain qui se cache sous le pseudonyme de Pierre de Corlay) "a-t-il traduit ainsi l'essence même de la fémininité: tendresse et coquetterie, pudeur et sourde volupté, tout le mystère d'un cœur qui se réserve, d'un cerveau qui réfléchit, d'une personnalité qui se garde et ne livre d'elle-même que son rayonnement. . . ."*'[1] The Italian writer Angelo Conti (1910, 93) saw the picture in the Louvre brought to life by a ray of sunshine. '*La donna sorrideva in una calma regale: i suoi istinti di conquista, di ferocia, tutta l'eredità della specie, la volontà della seduzione e dell'agguato, la grazia del inganno, la bontà che cela un proposito crudele, tutto ciò appariva alternativamente e scompariva dietro il velo ridente e si fondeva nel poema del suo sorriso. . . . Buona e malvagia, crudele e compassionevole, graziosa e felina, ella rideva. . . .*'[2]

Leonardo spent four years painting at this picture,

1. ['We know what an insoluble and enthralling enigma Mona Lisa Gioconda has never ceased through nearly four centuries to pose to the admirers that throng in front of her. No artist (I borrow the words from the sensitive writer who conceals himself behind the pseudonym of Pierre de Corlay) "has ever expressed so well the very essence of femininity: tenderness and coquetry, modesty and secret sensuous joy, all the mystery of a heart that holds aloof, a brain that meditates, a personality that holds back and yields nothing of itself save its radiance".']

2. ['The lady smiled in regal calm: her instincts of conquest, of ferocity, all the heredity of the species, the will to seduce and to ensnare, the charm of deceit, the kindness that conceals a cruel

perhaps from 1503 to 1507, during his second period of
residence in Florence, when he was over fifty. According
to Vasari he employed the most elaborate artifices to
keep the lady amused during the sittings and to retain
the famous smile on her features. In its present condition the picture has preserved but little of all the delicate details which his brush reproduced on the canvas
at that time; while it has being painted it was considered to be the highest that art could achieve, but it
is certain that Leonardo himself was not satisfied with
it, declaring it to be incomplete, and did not deliver it
to the person who had commissioned it, but took it to
France with him, where his patron, Francis I, acquired
it from him for the Louvre.

Let us leave unsolved the riddle of the expression on
Mona Lisa's face, and note the indisputable fact that
her smile exercised no less powerful a fascination on the
artist than on all who have looked at it for the last four
hundred years. From that date the captivating smile
reappears in all his pictures and in those of his pupils.
As Leonardo's 'Mona Lisa' is a portrait, we cannot
assume that he added on his own account such an
expressive feature to her face – a feature that she did
not herself possess. The conclusion seems hardly to be
avoided that he found this smile in his model and fell
so strongly under its spell that from then on he bestowed
it on the free creations of his phantasy. This interpretation, which cannot be called far-fetched, is put forward,
for example, by Konstantinowa (1907, 44):

'During the long period in which the artist was
occupied with the portrait of Mona Lisa del Giocondo,

purpose – all this appeared and disappeared by turns behind the
laughing veil and buried itself in the poem of her smile . . . Good
and wicked, cruel and compassionate, graceful and feline, she
laughed . . .']

LEONARDO

he had entered into the subtle details of the features on this lady's face with such sympathetic feeling that he transferred its traits – in particular the mysterious smile and the strange gaze – to all the faces that he painted or drew afterwards. The Gioconda's peculiar facial expression can even be perceived in the picture of John the Baptist in the Louvre; but above all it may be clearly recognized in the expression on Mary's face in the "Madonna and Child with St Anne".[1]

Yet this situation may also have come about in another way. The need for a deeper reason behind the attraction of La Gioconda's smile, which so moved the artist that he was never again free from it, has been felt by more than one of his biographers. Walter Pater, who sees in the picture of Mona Lisa a 'presence ... expressive of what in the ways of a thousand years men had come to desire' [1873, 118], and who writes very sensitively of 'the unfathomable smile, always with a touch of something sinister in it, which plays over all Leonardo's work' [ibid., 117], leads us to another clue when he declares (loc. cit.):

'Besides, the picture is a portrait. From childhood we see this image defining itself on the fabric of his dreams; and but for express historical testimony, we might fancy that this was but his ideal lady, embodied and beheld at last. ...'

Marie Herzfeld (1906, 88) has no doubt something very similar in mind when she declares that in the 'Mona Lisa' Leonardo encountered his own self and for this reason was able to put so much of his own nature into the picture 'whose features had lain all along in mysterious sympathy within Leonardo's mind'.

1. [The title of this subject in German is 'Heilige Anna Selbdritt', literally 'St Anne with Two Others', a point which is referred to below, p. 155.]

LEONARDO

Let us attempt to clarify what is suggested here. It may very well have been that Leonardo was fascinated by Mona Lisa's smile for the reason that it awoke something in him which had for long lain dormant in his mind – probably an old memory. This memory was of sufficient importance for him never to get free of it when it had once been aroused; he was continually forced to give it new expression. Pater's confident assertion that we can see, from childhood, a face like Mona Lisa's defining itself on the fabric of his dreams, seems convincing and deserves to be taken literally.

Vasari mentions that '*teste di femmine, che ridono*'[1] formed the subject of Leonardo's first artistic endeavours. The passage – which, since it is not intended to prove anything, is quite beyond suspicion – runs more fully according to Schorn's translation (1843, **3**, 6): 'In his youth he made some heads of laughing women out of clay, which were reproduced in plaster, and some children's heads which were as beautiful as if they had been modelled by the hand of a master. . . .'

Thus we learn that he began his artistic career by portraying two kinds of objects; and these cannot fail to remind us of the two kinds of sexual objects that we have inferred from the analysis of his vulture phantasy. If the beautiful children's heads were reproductions of his own person as it was in his childhood, then the smiling women are nothing other than repetitions of his mother Caterina, and we begin to suspect the possibility that it was his mother who possessed the mysterious smile – the smile that he had lost and that fascinated him so much when he found it again in the Florentine lady.[2]

1. ['Heads of laughing women.'] Quoted by Scognamiglio (1900, 32).
2. The same assumption is made by Merezhkovsky. But the history of Leonardo's childhood as he imagines it departs at the

The painting of Leonardo's which stands nearest to the 'Mona Lisa' in point of time is the so-called 'St Anne with Two Others', St Anne with the Madonna and Child. In it the Leonardesque smile is most beautifully and markedly portrayed on both the women's faces. It is not possible to discover how long before or after the painting of the 'Mona Lisa' Leonardo began to paint this picture. As both works extended over years, it may, I think, be assumed that the artist was engaged on them at the same time. It would best agree with our expectations if it was the intensity of Leonardo's preoccupation with the features of Mona Lisa which stimulated him to create the composition of St Anne out of his phantasy. For if the Gioconda's smile called up in his mind the memory of his mother, it is easy to understand how it drove him at once to create a glorification of motherhood, and to give back to his mother the smile he had found in the noble lady. We may therefore permit our interest to pass from Mona Lisa's portrait to this other picture – one which is hardly less beautiful, and which today also hangs in the Louvre.

St Anne with her daughter and her grandchild is a subject that is rarely handled in Italian painting. At all events Leonardo's treatment of it differs widely from all other known versions. Muther (1909, **I**, 309) writes:

'Some artists, like Hans Fries, the elder Holbein, and Girolamo dai Libri, made Anne sit beside Mary and put the child between them. Others, like Jakob Cornelisz in his Berlin picture, painted what was truly a "St Anne with Two Others";[1] in other words, they repre-

essential points from the conclusions we have drawn from the phantasy of the vulture. Yet if the smile had been that of Leonardo himself [as Merezhkovsky also assumes] tradition would hardly have failed to inform us of the coincidence.

1. [i.e., St Anne was the most prominent figure in the picture. See footnote, p. 153 above.]

sented her as holding in her arms the small figure of Mary upon which the still smaller figure of the child Christ is sitting.' In Leonardo's picture Mary is sitting on her mother's lap, leaning forward, and is stretching out both arms towards the boy, who is playing with a young lamb and perhaps treating it a little unkindly. The grandmother rests on her hip the arm that is not concealed and gazes down on the pair with a blissful smile. The grouping is certainly not entirely unconstrained. But although the smile that plays on the lips of the two women is unmistakably the same as that in the picture of Mona Lisa, it has lost its uncanny and mysterious character; what it expresses is inward feeling and quiet blissfulness.[1]

After we have studied this picture for some time, it suddenly dawns on us that only Leonardo could have painted it, just as only he could have created the phantasy of the vulture. The picture contains the synthesis of the history of his childhood: its details are to be explained by reference to the most personal impressions in Leonardo's life. In his father's house he found not only his kind stepmother, Donna Albiera, but also his grandmother, his father's mother, Monna Lucia, who – so we will assume – was no less tender to him than grandmothers usually are. These circumstances might well suggest to him a picture representing childhood watched over by mother and grandmother. Another striking feature of the picture assumes even greater significance. St Anne, Mary's mother and the boy's grandmother, who must have been a matron, is here portrayed

1. Konstantinowa (1907, [44]): 'Mary gazes down full of inward feeling on her darling, with a smile that recalls the mysterious expression of La Gioconda.' In another passage [ibid., 52] she says of Mary: 'The Gioconda's smile hovers on her features.'

as being perhaps a little more mature and serious than the Virgin Mary, but as still being a young woman of unfaded beauty. In point of fact Leonardo has given the boy two mothers, one who stretches her arms out to him, and another in the background; and both are endowed with the blissful smile of the joy of motherhood. This peculiarity of the picture has not failed to surprise those who have written about it: Muther, for example, is of the opinion that Leonardo could not bring himself to paint old age, lines, and wrinkles, and for this reason made Anne too into a woman of radiant beauty. But can we be satisfied with this explanation? Others have had recourse to denying that there is any similarity in age between the mother and daughter.[1] But Muther's attempt at an explanation is surely enough to prove that the impression that St Anne has been made more youthful derives from the picture and is not an invention for an ulterior purpose.

Leonardo's childhood was remarkable in precisely the same way as this picture. He had had two mothers: first, his true mother Caterina, from whom he was torn away when he was between three and five, and then a young and tender stepmother, his father's wife, Donna Albiera. By his combining this fact about his childhood with the one mentioned above (the presence of his mother and grandmother)[2] and by his condensing them into a composite unity, the design of 'St Anne with Two Others' took shape for him. The maternal figure that is further away from the boy – the grandmother – corresponds to the earlier and true mother, Caterina, in its appearance and in its special relation to the boy. The artist seems to have used the blissful smile of St Anne to disavow and to cloak the envy which the unfortunate

1. Von Seidlitz (1909, 2, 274, notes).
2. [The words in parentheses were added in 1923.]

woman felt when she was forced to give up her son to her better-born rival, as she had once given up his father as well.[1]

We thus find a confirmation in another of Leonardo's

1. [*Footnote added* 1919:] If an attempt is made to separate the figures of Anne and Mary in this picture and to trace the outline of each, it will not be found altogether easy. One is inclined to say that they are fused with each other like badly condensed dream-figures, so that in some places it is hard to say where Anne ends and where Mary begins. But what appears to a critic's eye [in 1919 only: 'to an artist's eye'] as a fault, as a defect in composition, is vindicated in the eyes of analysis by reference to its secret meaning. It seems that for the artist the two mothers of his childhood were melted into a single form.

[*Added* 1923:] It is especially tempting to compare the 'St Anne with Two Others' of the Louvre with the celebrated London cartoon, where the same material is used to form a different composition. [See Fig. 3] Here the forms of the two mothers are

FIG. 3

works of our suspicion that the smile of Mona Lisa del
Giocondo had awakened in him as a grown man the
memory of the mother of his earliest childhood. From
that time onward, madonnas and aristocratic ladies
were depicted in Italian painting humbly bowing their
heads and smiling the strange, blissful smile of Caterina,

---

fused even more closely and their separate outlines are even harder
to make out, so that critics, far removed from any attempt to offer
an interpretation, have been forced to say that it seems 'as if two
heads were growing from a single body'.

Most authorities are in agreement in pronouncing the London
cartoon to be the earlier work and in assigning its origin to
Leonardo's first period in Milan (before 1500). Adolf Rosenberg
(1898), on the other hand, sees the composition of the cartoon as
a later – and more successful – version of the same theme, and
follows Anton Springer in dating it even after the 'Mona Lisa'.
It would fit in excellently with our arguments if the cartoon were
to be much the earlier work. It is also not hard to imagine how the
picture in the Louvre arose out of the cartoon, while the reverse
course of events would make no sense. If we take the composition
shown in the cartoon as our starting-point, we can see how
Leonardo may have felt the need to undo the dream-like fusion of
the two women – a fusion corresponding to his childhood memory
– and to separate the two heads in space. This came about as
follows: From the group formed by the mothers he detached
Mary's head and the upper part of her body and bent them
downwards. To provide a reason for this displacement the child
Christ had to come down from her lap on to the ground. There was
then no room for the little St John, who was replaced by the lamb.

[*Added* 1919:] A remarkable discovery has been made in the
Louvre picture by Oskar Pfister, which is of undeniable interest,
even if one may not feel inclined to accept it without reserve. In
Mary's curiously arranged and rather confusing drapery he has
discovered the *outline of a vulture* and he interprets it as an *unconscious picture-puzzle*:

'In the picture that represents the artist's mother *the vulture, the
symbol of motherhood*, is perfectly clearly visible.

'In the length of blue cloth, which is visible around the hip of
the woman in front and which extends in the direction of her lap

the poor peasant girl who had brought into the world the splendid son who was destined to paint, to search, and to suffer.

———————

and her right knee, one can see the vulture's extremely characteristic head, its neck and the sharp curve where its body begins. Hardly any observer whom I have confronted with my little find has been able to resist the evidence of this picture-puzzle.' (Pfister, 1913, 147.)

At this point the reader will not, I feel sure, grudge the effort of looking at the accompanying illustration, to see if he can find in it the outlines of the vulture seen by Pfister. The piece of blue cloth, whose border marks the edges of the picture-puzzle, stands out in the reproduction as a light grey field against the darker ground of the rest of the drapery. [See Fig. 4.]

Fig. 4

Pfister continues: 'The important question however is: How far does the picture-puzzle extend? If we follow the length of cloth,

If Leonardo was successful in reproducing on Mona Lisa's face the double meaning which this smile contained, the promise of unbounded tenderness and at the same time sinister menace (to quote Pater's phrase [above, p. 153), then here too he had remained true to the content of his earliest memory. For his mother's tenderness was fateful for him; it determined his destiny and the privations that were in store for him. The violence of the caresses, to which his phantasy of the vulture points, was only too natural. In her love for her child the poor forsaken mother had to give vent to all her memories of the caresses she had enjoyed as well as her longing for new ones; and she was forced to do so not only to compensate herself for having no husband, but also to compensate her child for having no father to fondle him. So, like all unsatisfied mothers, she took her little son in place of her husband, and by the too early maturing of his erotism robbed him of a part of his masculinity. A mother's love for the infant she suckles and cares for is something far more profound than her later affection for the growing child. It is in the nature of a completely satisfying love-relation, which not only fulfils every mental wish but also every physical need;

which stands out so sharply from its surroundings, starting at the middle of the wing and continuing from there, we notice that one part of it runs down to the woman's foot, while the other part extends in an upward direction and rests on her shoulder and on the child. The former of these parts might more or less represent the vulture's wing and tail, as it is in nature; the latter might be a pointed belly and – especially when we notice the radiating lines which resemble the outlines of feathers – a bird's outspread tail, whose right-hand end, *exactly as in Leonardo's fateful childhood dream* [sic], *leads to the mouth of the child, i.e. of Leonardo himself.*'

The author goes on to examine the interpretation in greater detail, and discusses the difficulties to which it gives rise.

and if it represents one of the forms of attainable human happiness, that is in no little measure due to the possibility it offers of satisfying, without reproach, wishful impulses which have long been repressed and which must be called perverse.[1] In the happiest young marriage the father is aware that the baby, especially if he is a baby son, has become his rival, and this is the starting-point of an antagonism towards the favourite which is deeply rooted in the unconscious.

When, in the prime of life, Leonardo once more encountered the smile of bliss and rapture which had once played on his mother's lips as she fondled him, he had for long been under the dominance of an inhibition which forbade him ever again to desire such caresses from the lips of women. But he had become a painter, and therefore he strove to reproduce the smile with his brush, giving it to all his pictures (whether he in fact executed them himself or had them done by his pupils under his direction) – to 'Leda', to 'John the Baptist', and to 'Bacchus'. The last two are variants of the same type. 'Leonardo has turned the locust-eater of the Bible', says Muther [1909, **1**, 314], 'into a Bacchus, a young Apollo, who, with a mysterious smile on his lips, and with his smooth legs crossed, gazes at us with eyes that intoxicate the senses.' These pictures breathe a mystical air into whose secret one dares not penetrate; at the very most one can attempt to establish their connexion with Leonardo's earlier creations. The figures are still androgynous, but no longer in the sense of the vulture phantasy. They are beautiful youths of feminine delicacy and with effeminate forms; they do not cast their eyes down, but gaze in mysterious triumph, as if they knew of a great achievement of

1. See my *Three Essays on the Theory of Sexuality* (1905*a*) [*Standard Ed.*, **7**, 223].

happiness, about which silence must be kept. The familiar smile of fascination leads one to guess that it is a secret of love. It is possible that in these figures Leonardo has denied the unhappiness of his erotic life and has triumphed over it in his art, by representing the wishes of the boy, infatuated with his mother, as fulfilled in this blissful union of the male and female natures.

FIVE

Among the entries in Leonardo's notebooks there is one which catches the reader's attention owing to the importance of what it contains and to a minute formal error.

In July 1504 he writes:

'*Adì 9 di Luglio 1504 mercoledì a ore 7 morì Ser Piero da Vinci, notalio al palazzo del Potestà, mio padre, a ore 7. Era d'età d'anni 80, lascio 10 figlioli maschi e 2 femmine.*'[1]

As we see, the note refers to the death of Leonardo's father. The small error in its form consists of the repetition of the time of day '*a ore 7*' [at 7 o'clock], which is given twice, as if Leonardo had forgotten at the end of the sentence that he had already written it at the beginning. It is only a small detail, and anyone who was not a psycho-analyst would attach no importance to it. He might not even notice it, and if his attention was drawn to it he might say that a thing like that can happen to anyone in a moment of distraction or of strong feeling, and that it has no further significance.

The psycho-analyst thinks differently. To him nothing is too small to be a manifestation of hidden mental processes. He has learnt long ago that such cases of forgetting or repetition are significant, and that it is the 'distractions' which allows impulses that are otherwise hidden to be revealed.

We would say that this note, like the account for Caterina's funeral [p. 145] and the bills of the pupils'

1. ['On 9 July 1504, Wednesday at seven o'clock died Ser Piero da Vinci, notary at the palace of the Podestà, my father, at seven o'clock. He was eighty years old, and left ten sons and two daughters.'] After Müntz (1899, 13*n*.).

164

expenses [p. 144], is a case in which Leonardo was unsuccessful in suppressing his affect and in which something that had long been concealed forcibly obtained a distorted expression. Even the form is similar: there is the same pedantic exactness, and the same prominence given to numbers.[1]

We call a repetition of this kind a perseveration. It is an excellent means of indicating affective colour. One recalls, for example, St Peter's tirade in Dante's *Paradiso* against his unworthy representative on earth:

Quegli ch'usurpa in terra il luogo mio,
Il luogo mio, il luogo mio, che vaca
Nella presenza del Figliuol di Dio,

Fatto ha del cimiterio mio cloaca.[2]

Without Leonardo's affective inhibition the entry in his diary might have run somewhat as follows: 'Today at 7 o'clock my father died – Ser Piero da Vinci, my poor father!' But the displacement of the perseveration on to the most indifferent detail in the report of his death, the hour at which he died, robs the entry of all emotion, and further lets us see that here was something to be concealed and suppressed.

Ser Piero da Vinci, notary and descendant of notaries, was a man of great energy who reached a position of esteem and prosperity. He was married four times. His first two wives died childless, and it was only his third wife who presented him with his first legitimate son, in 1476, by which time Leonardo had reached the age of

1. I am leaving on one side a greater error made by Leonardo in this note by giving his father's age as eighty instead of seventy-seven. [See also note 1 on page 166.]

2. ['He who usurps on earth my place, my place, my place, which in the presence of the Son of God is vacant, has made a ewer of the ground where I am buried.'] Canto XXVII, 22–5.

twenty-four and had long ago exchanged his father's home for the studio of his master Verrocchio. By his fourth and last wife, whom he married when he was already in his fifties, he had nine more sons and two daughters.[1]

It cannot be doubted that his father too came to play an important part in Leonardo's psychosexual development, and not only negatively by his absence during the boy's first childhood years, but also directly by his presence in the later part of Leonardo's childhood. No one who as a child desires his mother can escape wanting to put himself in his father's place, can fail to identify himself with him in his imagination and later make it his task in life to gain ascendency over him. When Leonardo was received into his grandfather's house before he had reached the age of five, his young stepmother Albiera must certainly have taken his mother's place where his feelings were concerned, and he must have found himself in what may be called the normal relationship of rivalry with his father. As we know, a decision in favour of homosexuality only takes place round about the years of puberty. When this decision had been arrived at in Leonardo's case, his identification with his father lost all significance for his sexual life, but it nevertheless continued in other spheres of non-erotic activity. We hear that he was fond of magnificence and fine clothes, and kept servants and horses, although, in Vasari's words, 'he possessed almost nothing and did little work'. The responsibility for these tastes is not to be attributed solely to his feeling for beauty: we recognize in them at the same time a compulsion to copy and to outdo his father. His father had

1. Leonardo has apparently made a further mistake in this passage in his diary over the number of his brothers and sisters – a remarkable contrast to the apparent exactness of the passage.

been a great gentleman to the poor peasant girl, and the son, therefore, never ceased to feel the spur to play the great gentleman as well, the urge 'to out-herod Herod',[1] to show his father what a great gentleman really looks like.

There is no doubt that the creative artist feels towards his works like a father. The effect which Leonardo's identification with his father had on his paintings was a fateful one. He created them and then cared no more about them, just as his father had not cared about him. His father's later concern could change nothing in this compulsion; for the compulsion derived from the impressions of the first years of childhood, and what has been repressed and has remained unconscious cannot be corrected by later experiences.

In the days of the Renaissance – and even much later – every artist stood in need of a gentleman of rank, a benefactor and patron, who gave him commissions and in whose hands his fortune rested. Leonardo found his patron in Lodovico Sforza, called Il Moro, a man of ambition and a lover of splendour, astute in diplomacy, but of erratic and unreliable character. At his court in Milan Leonardo passed the most brilliant period of his life, and in his service his creative power attained its most uninhibited expansion, to which the 'Last Supper' and the equestrian statue of Francesco Sforza bore witness. He left Milan before catastrophe overtook Lodovico Sforza, who died a prisoner in a French dungeon. When the news of his patron's fate reached Leonardo, he wrote in his diary: 'The duke lost his dukedom and his property and his liberty, and none of the works that he undertook was completed.'[2]

1. [The last three words are in English in the original.]
2. '*Il duca perse lo stato e la roba e libertà e nessuna sua opera si finì per lui.*' Quoted by von Seidlitz (1909, **2**, 270).

It is remarkable, and certainly not without significance, that he here cast the same reproach at his patron which posterity was to bring against himself. It is as if he wanted to make someone from the class of his father's responsible for the fact that he himself left his works unfinished. In point of fact he was not wrong in what he said about the duke.

But if his imitation of his father did him damage as an artist, his rebellion against his father was the infantile determinant of what was perhaps an equally sublime achievement in the field of scientific research. In Merezhkovsky's admirable simile (1903, 348), he was like a man who had awoken too early in the darkness, while everyone else was still asleep. He dared to utter the bold assertion which contains within itself the justification for all independent research: '*He who appeals to authority when there is a difference of opinion works with his memory rather than with his reason.*'[1] Thus he became the first modern natural scientist, and an abundance of discoveries and suggestive ideas rewarded his courage for being the first man since the time of the Greeks to probe the secrets of nature while relying solely on observation and his own judgement. But in teaching that authority should be looked down on and that imitation of the 'ancients' should be repudiated, and in constantly urging that the study of nature was the source of all truth, he was merely repeating – in the highest sublimation attainable by man – the one-sided point of view which had already forced itself on the little boy as he gazed in wonder on the world. If we translate scientific abstraction back again into concrete individual experience, we see that the 'ancients' and authority simply correspond to his father, and nature

1. '*Chi disputa allegando l'autorità non adopra l'ingegno ma piuttosto la memoria.*' Quoted by Solmi (1910, 13). [*Codex Atlanticus*, F. 76 r.a.]

once more becomes the tender and kindly mother who had nourished him. In most other human beings – no less today than in primeval times – the need for support from an authority of some sort is so compelling that their world begins to totter if that authority is threatened. Only Leonardo could dispense with that support; he would not have been able to do so had he not learnt in the first years of his life to do without his father. His later scientific research, with all its boldness and independence, presupposed the existence of infantile sexual researches uninhibited by his father, and was a prolongation of them with the sexual element excluded.

When anyone has, like Leonardo, escaped being intimidated by his father during his earliest[1] childhood, and has in his researches cast away the fetters of authority, it would be in the sharpest contradiction to our expectation if we found that he had remained a believer and had been unable to escape from dogmatic religion. Psycho-analysis has made us familiar with the intimate connexion between the father-complex and belief in God; it has shown us that a personal God is, psychologically, nothing other than an exalted father, and it brings us evidence every day of how young people lose their religious beliefs as soon as their father's authority breaks down. Thus we recognize that the roots of the need for religion are in the parental complex; the almighty and just God, and kindly Nature, appear to us as grand sublimations of father and mother, or rather as revivals and restorations of the young child's ideas of them. Biologically speaking, religiousness is to be traced to the small human child's long-drawn-out helplessness and need of help; and when at a later date he perceives how truly forlorn and weak he is when

1. [This word was added in 1925.]

confronted with the great forces of life, he feels his condition as he did in childhood, and attempts to deny his own despondency by a regressive revival of the forces which protected his infancy. The protection against neurotic illness, which religion vouchsafes to those who believe in it, is easily explained: it removes their parental complex, on which the sense of guilt in individuals as well as in the whole human race depends, and disposes of it, while the unbeliever has to grapple with the problem on his own.[1]

It does not seem as if the instance of Leonardo could show this view of religious belief to be mistaken. Accusations charging him with unbelief or (what at that time came to the same thing) with apostasy from Christianity were brought against him while he was still alive, and are clearly described in the first biography which Vasari [1550] wrote of him. (Müntz, 1899, 292 ff.) In the second (1568) edition of his *Vite* Vasari omitted these observations. In view of the extraordinary sensitiveness of his age where religious matters were in question, we can understand perfectly why even in his notebooks Leonardo should have refrained from directly stating his attitude to Christianity. In his researches he did not allow himself to be led astray in the slightest degree by the account of the Creation in Holy Writ; he challenged, for example, the possibility of a universal Deluge, and in geology he calculated in terms of hundreds of thousands of years with no more hesitation than men in modern times.

Among his 'prophecies' there are some things that would have been bound to offend the sensitive feelings

---

1. [This last sentence was added in 1919. The same point is mentioned in Freud's contemporary address to the Nuremberg Congress (1910), and again, much later, in the last chapter of *Group Psychology* (1921), *Standard Ed.*, **18**, 142.]

of a Christian believer. Take for example, 'On the practice of praying to the images of saints':

'Men will speak to men that perceive nothing, that have their eyes open and see nothing; they will talk to them and receive no answer; they will implore the grace of those that have ears and hear not; they will kindle lights for one that is blind.' (After Herzfeld, 1906, 292.)

Or 'On the mourning on Good Friday':

'In every part of Europe great peoples will weep for the death of a single man who died in the East.' (Ibid., 297.)

The view has been expressed about Leonardo's art that he took from the sacred figures the last remnant of their connexion with the Church and made them human, so as to represent by their means great and beautiful human emotions. Muther praises him for overcoming the prevailing mood of decadence and for restoring to man his right to sensuality and the joy of living. In the notes that show Leonardo engrossed in fathoming the great riddles of nature there is no lack of passages where he expresses his admiration for the Creator, the ultimate cause of all these noble secrets; but there is nothing which indicates that he wished to maintain any personal relation with this divine power. The reflections in which he has recorded the deep wisdom of his last years of life breathe the resignation of the human being who subjects himself to Ἀνάγκη, to the laws of nature, and who expects no alleviation from the goodness or grace of God. There is scarcely any doubt that Leonardo had prevailed over both dogmatic and personal religion, and had by his work of research removed himself far from the position from which the Christian believer surveys the world.

The findings, mentioned above [p. 133 ff.], which we

have reached concerning the development of the mental life of children suggest the view that in Leonardo's case too the first researches of childhood were concerned with the problem of sexuality. Indeed he himself gives this away in a transparent disguise by connecting his urge for research with the vulture phantasy, and by singling out the problem of the flight of birds as one to which, as the result of a special chain of circumstances, he was destined to turn his attention. A highly obscure passage in his notes which is concerned with the flight of birds, and which sounds like a prophecy, gives a very good demonstration of the degree of affective interest with which he clung to his wish to succeed in imitating the art of flying himself: 'The great bird will take its first flight from the back of its Great Swan; it will fill the universe with stupefaction, and all writings with renown, and be the eternal glory of the nest where it was born.'[1] He probably hoped that he himself would be able to fly one day, and we know from wish-fulfilling dreams what bliss is expected from the fulfilment of that hope.

But why do so many people dream of being able to fly? The answer that psycho-analysis gives is that to fly or to be a bird is only a disguise for another wish, and that more than one bridge, involving words or things, leads us to recognize what it is. When we consider that inquisitive children are told that babies are brought by a large bird, such as the stork; when we find that the ancients represented the phallus as having wings; that the commonest expression in German for male sexual activity is '*vögeln*' ['to bird': '*Vogel*' is the German for 'bird']; that the male organ is actually called '*l'uccello*'

---

1. After Herzfeld (1906, 32). 'The Great Swan' seems to mean Monte Cecero, a hill near Florence [now Monte Ceceri: '*Cecero*' is Italian for 'swan'].

['the bird'] in Italian – all of these are only small frag-
ments from a whole mass of connected ideas, from which
we learn that in dreams the wish to be able to fly is to
be understood as nothing else than a longing to be
capable of sexual performance.[1] This is an early infantile wish. When an adult recalls his childhood it seems
to him to have been a happy time, in which one enjoyed
the moment and looked to the future without any
wishes; it is for this reason that he envies children. But
if children themselves were able to give us information
earlier[2] they would probably tell a different story. It
seems that childhood is not the blissful idyll into which
we distort it in retrospect, and that, on the contrary,
children are goaded on through the years of childhood
by the one wish to get big and do what grown-ups do.
This wish is the motive of all their games. Whenever
children feel in the course of their sexual researches that
in the province which is so mysterious but nevertheless
so important there is something wonderful of which
adults are capable but which *they* are forbidden to know
of and do, they are filled with a violent wish to be able
to do it, and they dream of it in the form of flying, or
they prepare this disguise of their wish to be used in
their later flying dreams. Thus aviation, too, which in
our day is at last achieving its aim, has its infantile
erotic roots.

In admitting to us that ever since his childhood he
felt bound up in a special and personal way with the

1. [*Footnote added* 1919:] This statement is based on the researches of Paul Federn [1914] and of Mourly Vold (1912), a
Norwegian man of science who had no contact with psycho-
analysis. [See also *The Interpretation of Dreams* (1900), *Standard Ed.*,
5, 394.]

2. ['*Früher*.' In the editions before 1923 '*darüber*' appears in
place of '*früher*', giving the meaning 'about it'.]

problem of flight, Leonardo gives us confirmation that his childhood researches were directed to sexual matters; and this is what we were bound to expect as a result of our investigations on children in our own time. Here was one problem at least which had escaped the repression that later estranged him from sexuality. With slight changes in meaning, the same subject continued to interest him from his years of childhood until the time of his most complete intellectual maturity; and it may very well be that the skill that he desired was no more attainable by him in its primary sexual sense than in its mechanical one, and that he remained frustrated in both wishes.

Indeed, the great Leonardo remained like a child for the whole of his life in more than one way; it is said that all great men are bound to retain some infantile part. Even as an adult he continued to play, and this was another reason why he often appeared uncanny and incomprehensible to his contemporaries. It is only we who are unsatisfied that he should have constructed the most elaborate mechanical toys for court festivities and ceremonial receptions, for we are reluctant to see the artist turning his power to such trifles. He himself seems to have shown no unwillingness to spend his time thus, for Vasari tells us that he made similar things when he had not been commissioned to do so: 'There (in Rome) he got a soft lump of wax, and made very delicate animals out of it, filled with air; when he blew into them they flew around, and when the air ran out they fell to the ground. For a peculiar lizard which was found by the wine-grower of Belvedere he made wings from skin torn from other lizards, and filled them with quicksilver, so that they moved and quivered when it walked. Next he made eyes, a beard, and horns for it, tamed it, and put it in a box and terrified all his friends with it.'[1] Such ingenuities often served to express thoughts of a serious kind. 'He often had a sheep's intestines cleaned so carefully that they could have been held in the hollow of the hand. He carried them into a large room, took a pair of blacksmith's bellows into an adjoining room, fastened the intestines to them and blew them up, until they took up the whole room and forced people to take refuge in a corner. In this way he showed how they gradually became transparent and filled with air; and from the fact that at first they were limited to a small space and gradually spread through the whole breadth of the room, he compared them to genius.'[2] The same playful delight in harmlessly concealing things and giving them ingenious disguises is illustrated by his fables and riddles. The latter are cast into the form of 'prophecies': almost all are rich in ideas and to a striking degree devoid of any element of wit.

The games and pranks which Leonardo allowed his imagination have in some cases led his biographers, who misunderstood this side of his character, grievously astray. In Leonardo's Milanese manuscripts there are, for example, some drafts of letters to the 'Diodario of Sorio (Syria), Viceroy of the Holy Sultan of Babylonia', in which Leonardo presents himself as an engineer sent to those regions of the East to construct certain works; defends himself against the charge of laziness; supplies geographical descriptions of towns and mountains; and concludes with an account of a great natural phenomenon that occurred while he was there.[3]

1. Vasari, from Schorn's translation (1843, 39) [ed. Poggi, 1919, 41].
2. Ibid., 39 [ed. Poggi, 41].
3. For these letters and the various questions connected with them see Müntz (1899, 82 ff.); the actual texts and other related notes will be found in Herzfeld (1906, 223 ff.).

In 1883 an attempt was made by J. P. Richter to prove from these documents that it was really a fact that Leonardo had made these observations while travelling in the service of the Sultan of Egypt, and had even adopted the Mohammedan religion when in the East. On this view his visit there took place in the period before 1483 – that is, before he took up residence at the court of the Duke of Milan. But the acumen of other authors has had no difficulty in recognizing the evidences of Leonardo's supposed Eastern journey for what they are – imaginary productions of the youthful artist, which he created for his own amusement and in which he may have found expression for a wish to see the world and meet with adventures.

Another probable example of a creation of his imagination is to be found in the 'Academia Vinciana' which has been postulated from the existence of five or six emblems, intertwined patterns of extreme intricacy, which contain the Academy's name. Vasari mentions these designs but not the Academy.[1] Müntz, who put one of these ornaments on the cover of his large work on Leonardo, is among the few who believe in the reality of an 'Academia Vinciana'.

It is probable that Leonardo's play-instinct vanished in his maturer years, and that it too found its way into the activity of research which represented the latest and highest expansion of his personality. But its long duration can teach us how slowly anyone tears himself from his childhood if in his childhood days he has enjoyed the highest erotic bliss, which is never again attained.

1. 'Besides, he lost some time by even making a drawing of knots of cords, in which it was possible to trace the thread from one end to the other, until it formed a completely circular figure. A very complex and beautiful design of this sort is engraved on copper; in the middle can be read the words *Leonardus Vinci Academia*.' Schorn (1843, 8) [ed. Poggi, 5].

SIX

IT would be futile to blind ourselves to the fact that readers today find all pathography unpalatable. They clothe their aversion in the complaint that a pathographical review of a great man never results in an understanding of his importance and his achievements, and that it is therefore a piece of useless impertinence to make a study of things in him that could just as easily be found in the first person one came across. But this criticism is so manifestly unjust that it is only understandable when taken as a pretext and a disguise. Pathography does not in the least aim at making the great man's achievements intelligible; and surely no one should be blamed for not carrying out something he has never promised to do. The real motives for the opposition are different. We can discover them if we bear in mind that biographers are fixated on their heroes in a quite special way. In many cases they have chosen their hero as the subject of their studies because – for reasons of their personal emotional life – they have felt a special affection for him from the very first. They then devote their energies to a task of idealization, aimed at enrolling the great man among the class of their infantile models – at reviving in him, perhaps, the child's idea of his father. To gratify this wish they obliterate the individual features of their subject's physiognomy; they smooth over the traces of his life's struggles with internal and external resistances, and they tolerate in him no vestige of human weakness or imperfection. They thus present us with what is in fact a cold, strange, ideal figure, instead of a human being to whom we might feel ourselves distantly related. That they should do this is regrettable, for they thereby sacrifice truth to an illusion, and for the sake of their infantile phantasies abandon the opportunity of penetrating the most fascinating secrets of human nature.[1]

Leonardo himself, with his love of truth and his thirst for knowledge, would not have discouraged an attempt to take the trivial peculiarities and riddles in his nature as a starting-point for discovering what determined his mental and intellectual development. We do homage to him by learning from him. It does not detract from his greatness if we make a study of the sacrifices which his development from childhood must have entailed, and if we bring together the factors which have stamped him with the tragic mark of failure.

We must expressly insist that we have never reckoned Leonardo as a neurotic or a 'nerve case', as the awkward phrase goes. Anyone who protests at our so much as daring to examinine him in the light of discoveries gained in the field of pathology is still clinging to prejudices which we have today rightly abandoned. We no longer think that health and illness, normal and neurotic people, are to be sharply distinguished from each other, and that neurotic traits must necessarily be taken as proofs of a general inferiority. Today we know that neurotic symptoms are structures which are substitutes for certain achievements of repression that we have to carry out in the course of our development from a child to a civilized human being. We know too that we all produce such substitutive structures, and that it is only their number, intensity, and distribution which justify us in using the practical concept of illness and in inferring the presence of constitutional inferiority. From the slight indications we have about Leonardo's

1. This criticism applies quite generally and is not to be taken as being aimed at Leonardo's biographers in particular.

personality we should be inclined to place him close to the type of neurotic that we describe as 'obsessional'; and we may compare his researches to the 'obsessive brooding' of neurotics, and his inhibitions to what are known as their 'abulias'.

The aim of our work has been to explain the inhibitions in Leonardo's sexual life and in his artistic activity. With this in view we may be allowed to summarize what we have been able to discover about the course of his psychical development.

We have no information about the circumstances of his heredity; on the other hand we have seen that the accidental conditions of his childhood had a profound and disturbing effect on him. His illegitimate birth deprived him of his father's influence until perhaps his fifth year, and left him open to the tender seductions of a mother whose only solace he was. After being kissed by her into precocious sexual maturity, he must no doubt have embarked on a phase of infantile sexual activity of which only one single manifestation is definitely attested – the intensity of his infantile sexual researches. The instinct to look and the instinct to know were those most strongly excited by the impressions of his early childhood; the erotogenic zone of the mouth was given an emphasis which it never afterwards surrendered. From his later behaviour in the contrary direction, such as his exaggerated sympathy for animals, we can conclude that there was no lack of strong sadistic traits in this period of his childhood.

A powerful wave of repression brought this childhood excess to an end, and established the dispositions which were to become manifest in the years of puberty. The most obvious result of the transformation was the avoidance of every crudely sensual activity; Leonardo was enabled to live in abstinence and to give the impression of being an asexual human being. When the excitations of puberty came in their flood upon the boy they did not, however, make him ill by forcing him to develop substitutive structures of a costly and harmful kind. Owing to his very early inclination towards sexual curiosity the greater portion of the needs of his sexual instinct could be sublimated into a general urge to know, and thus evaded repression. A much smaller portion of his libido continued to be devoted to sexual aims and represented a stunted adult sexual life. Because his love for his mother had been repressed, this portion was driven to take up a homosexual attitude and manifested itself in ideal love for boys. The fixation on his mother and on the blissful memories of his relations with her continued to be preserved in the unconscious, but for the time being it remained in an inactive state. In this way, repression, fixation, and sublimation all played their part in disposing of the contributions which the sexual instinct made to Leonardo's mental life.

Leonardo emerges from the obscurity of his boyhood as an artist, a painter, and a sculptor, owing to a specific talent which may have been reinforced by the precocious awakening in the first years of childhood of his scopophilic instinct. We should be most glad to give an account of the way in which artistic activity derives from the primal instincts of the mind if it were not just here that our capacities fail us. We must be content to emphasize the fact – which it is hardly any longer possible to doubt – that what an artist creates provides at the same time an outlet for his sexual desire; and in Leonardo's case we can point to the information which comes from Vasari [above p. 154], that heads of laughing women and beautiful boys – in other words, representations of his sexual objects – were notable among his first artistic endeavours. In the bloom of his youth

Leonardo appears at first to have worked without inhibition. Just as he modelled himself on his father in the outward conduct of his life, so too he passed through a period of masculine creative power and artistic productiveness in Milan, where a kindly fate enabled him to find a father-substitute in the duke Lodovico Moro. But soon we find confirmation of our experience that the almost total repression of a real sexual life does not provide the most favourable conditions for the exercise of sublimated sexual trends. The pattern imposed by sexual life made itself felt. His activity and his ability to form quick decisions began to fail; his tendency towards deliberation and delay was already noticeable as a disturbing element in the 'Last Supper', and by influencing his technique it had a decisive effect on the fate of that great painting. Slowly there occurred in him a process which can only be compared to the regressions in neurotics. The development that turned him into an artist at puberty was overtaken by the process which led him to be an investigator, and which had its determinants in early infancy. The second sublimation of his erotic instinct gave place to the original sublimation for which the way had been prepared on the occasion of the first repression. He became an investigator, at first still in the service of his art, but later independently of it and away from it. With the loss of his patron, the substitute for his father, and with the increasingly sombre colours which his life took on, this regressive shift assumed larger and larger proportions. He became 'impacientissimo al pennello',[1] as we are told by a correspondent of the Countess Isabella d'Este, who was extremely eager to possess a painting from his hand. His infantile past had gained control over him. But the research which now took the place of artistic creation

1. ['Very impatient of painting.'] Von Seidlitz (1909, 2, 271).

seems to have contained some of the features which distinguish the activity of unconscious instincts – insatiability, unyielding rigidity, and the lack of an ability to adapt to real circumstances.

At the summit of his life, when he was in his early fifties – a time when in women the sexual characters have already undergone involution and when in men the libido not infrequently makes a further energetic advance – a new transformation came over him. Still deeper layers of the contents of his mind became active once more, but this further regression was to the benefit of his art, which was in the process of becoming stunted. He met the woman who awakened his memory of his mother's happy smile of sensual rapture; and, influenced by this revived memory, he recovered the stimulus that guided him at the beginning of his artistic endeavours, at the time when he modelled the smiling women. He painted the 'Mona Lisa', the 'St Anne with Two Others', and the series of mysterious pictures which are characterized by the enigmatic smile. With the help of the oldest of all his erotic impulses he enjoyed the triumph of once more conquering the inhibition in his art. This final development is obscured from our eyes in the shadows of approaching age. Before this his intellect had soared upwards to the highest realizations of a conception of the world that left his epoch far behind it.

In the preceding chapters I have shown what justification can be found for giving this picture of Leonardo's course of development – for proposing these subdivisions of his life and for explaining his vacillation between art and science in this way. If in making these statements I have provoked the criticism, even from friends of psycho-analysis and from those who are expert in it, that I have merely written a psycho-analytic novel, I shall reply that I am far from over-estimating the certainty of these results. Like others, I have succumbed to the attraction of this great and mysterious man, in whose nature one seems to detect powerful instinctual passions which can nevertheless only express themselves in so remarkably subdued a manner.

But whatever the truth about Leonardo's life may be, we cannot desist from our endeavour to find a psychoanalytic explanation for it until we have completed another task. We must stake out in a quite general way the limits which are set to what psycho-analysis can achieve in the field of biography: otherwise every explanation that is not forthcoming will be held up to us as a failure. The material at the disposal of a psychoanalytic inquiry consists of the data of a person's life history: on the one hand the chance circumstances of events and background influences, and on the other hand the subject's reported reactions. Supported by its knowledge of psychical mechanisms it then endeavours to establish a dynamic basis for his nature on the strength of his reactions, and to disclose the original motive forces of his mind, as well as their later transformations and developments. If this is successful the behaviour of a personality in the course of his life is explained in terms of the combined operation of constitution and fate, of internal forces and external powers. Where such an undertaking does not provide any certain results – and this is perhaps so in Leonardo's case – the blame rests not with the faulty or inadequate methods of psycho-analysis, but with the uncertainty and fragmentary nature of the material relating to him which tradition makes available. It is therefore only the author who is to be held responsible for the failure, by having forced psycho-analysis to pronounce an expert opinion on the basis of such insufficient material.

But even if the historical material at our disposal were

very abundant, and if the psychical mechanisms could be dealt with with the greatest assurance, there are two important points at which a psycho-analytic inquiry would not be able to make us understand how inevitable it was that the person concerned should have turned out in the way he did and in no other way. In Leonardo's case we have had to maintain the view that the accident of his illegitimate birth and the excessive tenderness of his mother had the most decisive influence on the formation of his character and on his later fortune, since the sexual repression which set in after this phase of childhood caused him to sublimate his libido into the urge to know, and established his sexual inactivity for the whole of his later life. But this repression after the first erotic satisfactions of childhood need not necessarily have taken place; in someone else it might perhaps not have taken place or might have assumed much less extensive proportions. We must recognize here a degree of freedom which cannot be resolved any further by psycho-analytic means. Equally, one has no right to claim that the consequence of his wave of repression was the only possible one. It is probable that another person would not have succeeded in withdrawing the major portion of his libido from repression by sublimating it into a craving for knowledge; under the same influences he would have sustained a permanent injury to his intellectual activity or have acquired an insurmountable disposition to obsessional neurosis. We are left, then, with these two characteristics of Leonardo which are inexplicable by the efforts of psycho-analysis: his quite special tendency towards instinctual repressions, and his extraordinary capacity for sublimating the primitive instincts.

Instincts and their transformations are at the limit of what is discernible by psycho-analysis. From that point it gives place to biological research. We are obliged to look for the source of the tendency to repression and the capacity for sublimation in the organic foundations of character on which the mental structure is only afterwards erected. Since artistic talent and capacity are intimately connected with sublimation we must admit that the nature of the artistic function is also inaccessible to us along psycho-analytic lines. The tendency of biological research today is to explain the chief features in a person's organic constitution as being the result of the blending of male and female dispositions, based on [chemical] substances. Leonardo's physical beauty and his left-handedness might be quoted in support of this view.[1] We will not, however, leave the ground of purely psychological research. Our aim remains that of demonstrating the connexion along the path of instinctual activity between a person's external experiences and his reactions. Even if psycho-analysis does not throw light on the fact of Leonardo's artistic power, it at least renders its manifestations and its limitations intelligible to us. It seems at any rate as if only a man who had had Leonardo's childhood experiences could have painted the 'Mona Lisa' and the 'St Anne', have secured so melancholy a fate for his works, and have embarked on such an astonishing career as a natural scientist, as if the key to all his achievements and misfortunes lay hidden in the childhood phantasy of the vulture.

But may one not take objection to the findings of an inquiry which ascribes to accidental circumstances of

1. [This is no doubt an allusion to the views of Fliess by which Freud had been greatly influenced. Cf. his *Three Essays* (1905*a*), *Standard Ed.*, **7**, 216*n*. On the particular question of bilaterality, however, they had not been in complete agreement. See above, p. 7*n*.]

his parental constellation so decisive an influence on a person's fate – which, for example, makes Leonardo's fate depend on his illegitimate birth and on the barrenness of his first stepmother Donna Albiera? I think one has no right to do so. If one considers chance to be unworthy of determining our fate, it is simply a relapse into the pious view of the Universe which Leonardo himself was on the way to overcoming when he wrote that the sun does not move [p. 110]. We naturally feel hurt that a just God and a kindly providence do not protect us better from such influences during the most defenceless period of our lives. At the same time we are all too ready to forget that in fact everything to do with our life is chance, from our origin out of the meeting of spermatozoon and ovum onwards – chance which nevertheless has a share in the law and necessity of nature, and which merely lacks any connexion with our wishes and illusions. The apportioning of the determining factors of our life between the 'necessities' of our constitution and the 'chances' of our childhood may still be uncertain in detail; but in general it is no longer possible to doubt the importance precisely of the first years of our childhood. We all still show too little respect for Nature which (in the obscure words of Leonardo which recall Hamlet's lines) 'is full of countless causes ['*ragioni*'] that never enter experience'.[1]

Every one of us human beings corresponds to one of the countless experiments in which these *ragioni* of nature force their way into experience.

1. '*La natura è piena d'infinite ragioni che non furono mai in isperienza*' (Herzfeld, 1906, 11). [The allusion seems to be to Hamlet's familiar words:
    There are more things in heaven and earth, Horatio,
    Than are dreamt of in your philosophy.]

BIBLIOGRAPHY

BOTTAZZI, F. (1910) 'Leonardo biologico e anatomico', *Conferenze Fiorentine*, Milan, 181.

BREUER, J., and FREUD, S. (1893). See FREUD, S. (1893) (1895).

CONFERENZE FIORENTINE (1910) *Leonardo da Vinci: Conferenze Fiorentine*, Milan.

CONTI, A. (1910) 'Leonardo pittore', *Conferenze Fiorentine*, Milan, 81.

ELLIS, HAVELOCK (1910) Review of S. Freud's *Eine Kindheitserinnerung des Leonardo da Vinci*, *J. Ment. Sci.*, **56**, 522.

FEDERN, P. (1914) 'Über zwei typische Traumensationen', *Jb. Psychoan.*, **6**, 89.
[*Trans.*: (In part) 'On Dreams of Flying', *Psycho-analytic Reader*, 1 (1948), 386.]

FREUD, S. (1893) with BREUER, J. 'Über den psychischen Mechanismus hysterischer Phänomene: Vorläufige Mitteilung', *G.S.*, **1**, 7; *G.W.*, **1**, 81.
[*Trans.*: 'On the Psychical Mechanism of Hysterical Phenomena: Preliminary Communication', *C.P.*, **1**, 24; *Standard Ed.*, **2**, 3.]

(1895) With BREUER, J. *Studien über Hysterie*, Vienna. *G.S.*, **1**, 3; *G.W.*, **1**, 77 (omitting Breuer's contributions).
[*Trans.*: *Studies on Hysteria*, *Standard Ed.*, **2**, including Breuer's contributions.]

(1900) *Die Traumdeutung*, Vienna. *G.S.*, 2–3; *G.W.*, 2–3.
[*Trans.*: *The Interpretation of Dreams*, London and New York, 1955; *Standard Ed.*, 4–5.]

(1901) *Zur Psychopathologie des Alltagslebens*, Berlin, 1904. *G.S.*, **4**, 3; *G.W.*, **4**.

[*Trans.*: *The Psychopathology of Everyday Life*, Standard Ed., **6**.]

(1905*a*) *Drei Abhandlungen zur Sexualtheorie*, Vienna. *G.S.*, **5**, 3; *G.W.*, **5**, 29.
[*Trans.*: *Three Essays on the Theory of Sexuality*, London, 1949; *Standard Ed.*, **7**, 125.]

(1905*b* [1901]) 'Bruchstück einer Hysterie-Analyse', *G.S.*, **8**, 3; *G.W.*, **5**, 163.
[*Trans.*: 'Fragment of an Analysis of a Case of Hysteria', *C.P.*, **3**, 13; *Standard Ed.*, **7**, 3.]

(1907) Antwort auf eine Rundfrage *Vom Lesen und von guten Büchern*, Vienna.
[*Trans.*: Contribution to a Questionnaire on Reading, *Int. J. Psycho-Anal.*, **32**, 319; *Standard Ed.*, **9**.]

(1908*a*) 'Charakter und Analterotik', *G.S.*, **5**, 261; *G.W.*, **7**, 203.
[*Trans.*: 'Character and Anal Erotism', *C.P.*, **2**, 45; *Standard Ed.*, **9**.]

(1908*b*) 'Über infantile Sexualtheorien', *G.S.*, **5**, 168; *G.W.*, **7**, 171.
[*Trans.*: 'On the Sexual Theories of Children', *C.P.*, **2**, 59; *Standard Ed.*, **9**.]

(1909) 'Analyse der Phobie eines fünfjährigen Knaben', *G.S.*, **8**, 129; *G.W.*, **7**, 243.
[*Trans.*: 'Analysis of a Phobia in a Five-Year-Old Boy', *C.P.*, **3**, 149; *Standard Ed.*, **10**, 3.]

(1901) 'Die zukünftigen Chancen der psychoanalytischen Therapie', *G.S.*, **6**, 25; *G.W.*, **8**, 104.
[*Trans.*: 'The Future Prospects of Psycho-Analytic Therapy', *C.P.*, **2**, 285; *Standard Ed.*, **11**, 141.]

(1914) 'Zur Einführung des Narzissmus', *G.S.*, **6**, 155; *G.W.*, **10**, 138.
[*Trans.*: 'On Narcissism: an Introduction', *C.P.*, **4**, 30; *Standard Ed.*, **14**, 69.]

(1917) 'Eine Kindheitserinnerung aus *Dichtung und Wahrheit*', *G.S.*, **10**, 357; *G.W.*, **12**, 15.
[*Trans.*: 'A Childhood Recollection from *Dichtung und Wahrheit*', *C.P.*, **4**, 357; *Standard Ed.*, **17**, 147.]

(1920*a*) 'Über die Psychogenese eines Falles von weiblicher Homosexualität', *G.S.*, **5**, 312; *G.W.*, **12**, 271.

[*Trans.*: 'The Psychogenesis of a Case of Female Homosexuality', *C.P.*, **2**, 202; *Standard Ed.*, **18**, 147.]

(1920*b*) *Jenseits des Lustprinzips*, Vienna. *G.S.*, **6**, 191; *G.W.*, **13**, 3.

[*Trans.*: *Beyond the Pleasure Principle*, London, 1950; *Standard Ed.*, **18**, 3.]

(1921) *Massenpsychologie und Ich-Analyse*, Vienna. *G.S.*, **6**, 261; *G.W.*, **13**, 73.

[*Trans.*: *Group Psychology and the Analysis of the Ego*, London, 1922; New York, 1940; *Standard Ed.*, **18**, 67.]

(1922) 'Über einige neurotische Mechanismen bei Eifersucht, Paranoia und Homosexualität', *G.S.*, **5**, 387; *G.W.*, **13**, 195.

[*Trans.*: 'Some Neurotic Mechanisms in Jealousy, Paranoia and Homosexuality', *C.P.*, **2**, 232; *Standard Ed.*, **18**, 223.]

(1939 [1937–9]) *Der Mann Moses und die monotheistische Religion*, *G.W.*, **16**, 103.

[*Trans.*: *Moses and Monotheism*, London and New York, 1939; *Standard Ed.*, **23**.]

(1950 [1887–1902]) *Aus den Anfängen der Psychoanalyse*, London. Includes 'Entwurf einer Psychologie' (1895).

[*Trans.*: *The Origins of Psycho-Analysis*, London and New York, 1954. Partly including 'A Project for a Scientific Psychology', in *Standard Ed.*, **1**.]

(1955 [1907–8]) Original Record of the Case of Obsessional Neuroses (the 'Rat Man'), *Standard Ed.*, **10**, 259. German text unpublished.

GARDINER, Sir A. (1950) *Egyptian Grammar* (2nd ed.), London.

HARTLEBEN, H. (1906) *Champollion, sein Leben und sein Werk*. Berlin.

HERZFELD, M. (1906) *Leonardo da Vinci: Der Denker*,

Forscher und Poet: Nach den veröffentlichten Handschriften (2nd ed.), Jena.

HORAPOLLO, *Hieroglyphica.* See LEEMANS, C. (1835).

JONES, E. (1955) *Sigmund Freud: Life and Work*, Vol. 2, London and New York.

JUNG, C. G. (1901) 'Über Konflikte der kindlichen Seele', *Jb. psychoan. psychopath. Forsch.*, **2**, 33.

KNIGHT, R. P. (1786) *A Discourse on the Worship of Priapus*, London.

[*French Trans.:* Le culte du Priape, Brussels, 1866.]

KONSTANTINOWA, A. (1907) *Die Entwickelung des Madonnentypus bei Leonardo da Vinci*, Strasbourg. (*Zur Kunstgeschichte des Auslandes*, Heft 54.)

KRAFFT-EBING, R. VON (1893) *Psychopathia Sexualis* (8th ed.), Stuttgart.

[*Trans.:* Psychopathia Sexualis, New York, 1922.]

LANZONE, R. (1861–6) *Dizionario di mitologia egizia* (5 vols.), Turin.

LEEMANS, C. (1835) (ed.) *Horapollonis Niloï Hieroglyphica*, Amsterdam.

LEONARDO DA VINCI, *Codex Atlanticus*, Ambrosian Library, Milan, Publ. Giovanni Piumati, Milan, 1894–1904.

Quaderni d'Anatomia, Royal Library, Windsor. Catalogued Sir Kenneth Clark, Cambridge, 1935.

Trattato della Pittura, Vatican Library. See LUDWIG, H. (1909).

LUDWIG, H. (1909) German translation of Leonardo da Vinci's *Trattato della Pittura* under the title *Traktat von der Malerei* (2nd ed.), Jena.

MEREZHKOVSKY, D. S. (1895) *Smert Bogov*, St Petersburg.

[*Trans.:* The Death of the Gods, London, 1901.]

(1902) *Voskresenie Bogi*, St Petersburg.

[*Trans.:* The Forerunner, London, 1902. *Also: The Romance of Leonardo da Vinci*, London, 1903.]

[*German Trans.:* Leonardo da Vinci, Leipzig, 1903.]

(1905) *Antikhrist: Peter i Aleksyey*, St Petersburg.

EDITOR'S NOTE

THAT Freud's interest in Leonardo was of long standing is shown by a sentence in a letter to Fliess of 9 October 1898 (Freud, 1950,[1] Letter 98), in which he remarked that 'perhaps the most famous left-handed individual was Leonardo, who is not known to have had any love-affairs'.[2] This interest, furthermore, was not a passing one, for we find in Freud's reply to a 'questionnaire' on his favourite books (1907) that he mentions among them Merezhkovsky's study of Leonardo. But the immediate stimulus to writing the present work appears to have come in the autumn of 1909 from one of his patients who, as he remarked in a letter to Jung on 17 October, seemed to have the same constitution as Leonardo without his genius. He added that he was obtaining a book on Leonardo's youth from Italy. This was the monograph by Scognamiglio referred to on p. 118n. After reading this and some other books on Leonardo, he spoke on the subject to the Vienna Psycho-Analytical Society on 1 December; but it was not until the beginning of April 1910, that he finished writing his study. It was published at the end of May.

Freud made a number of corrections and additions in the later issues of the book. Among these may be specially mentioned the short footnote on circumcision (p. 134), the excerpt from Reitler (pp. 100–4n.), and the long quotation from Pfister (pp. 159–60n.), all of them added in 1919, and the discussion of the London cartoon (pp. 158–9n.), added in 1923.

This work of Freud's was not the first application of the methods of clinical psycho-analysis to the lives of historical figures in the past. Experiments in this direction had already been made by others, notably by Sadger, who had published studies on Conrad Ferdinand Meyer (1908), Lenau (1909), and Kleist (1909).[3]

1. See Bibliography for details of this and similar references.
2. A connexion between bilaterality and bisexuality had been asserted by Fliess but questioned by Freud. An indirect reference to this controversy (which was one of the occasions for their estrangement) will be found on p. 185 below.
3. The minutes of the Vienna Psycho-Analytical Society (which we are unfortunately precluded from quoting) show that at a meeting on 11 December 1907, Freud made some remarks on the subject of psycho-analytic biography. (Cf. Jones, 1955, 383.)

Freud himself had never before embarked on a full-length biographical study of this kind, though he had previously made a few fragmentary analyses of writers, based on episodes in their works. Long before this, in fact on 20 June 1898, he had sent Fliess a study of one of C. F. Meyer's short stories, *Die Richterin*, which threw light on its author's early life (Freud, 1950, Letter 91). But this monograph on Leonardo was not only the first but the last of Freud's large-scale excursions into the field of biography. The book seems to have been greeted with more than the usual amount of disapproval, and Freud was evidently justified in defending himself in advance with the reflections at the beginning of Chapter Six (p. 177) – reflections which have a general application even today to the authors and critics of biographies.

It is a strange fact, however, that until very recently none of the critics of the present work seems to have lighted upon what is no doubt its weakest point. A prominent part is played by Leonardo's memory or phantasy of being visited in his cradle by a bird of prey. The name applied to this bird in his notebooks is '*nibio*', which (in the modern form of '*nibbio*') is the ordinary Italian word for 'kite'. Freud, however, throughout his study translates the word by the German '*Geier*', for which the English can only be 'vulture'.[1]

Freud's mistake seems to have originated from some of the German translations which he used. Thus Marie Herzfeld (1906) uses the word '*Geier*' in one of her versions of the cradle phantasy instead of '*Milan*', the normal German word for 'kite'. But probably the most important influence was the German translation of Merezhkovsky's Leonardo book which, as may be seen from the marked copy in Freud's library, was the source of a very great deal of his information about Leonardo and in which he probably came across the story for the first time. Here too the German word used in the cradle phantasy is '*Geier*', though Merezhkovsky himself correctly used '*korshun*', the Russian word for 'kite'.

In face of this mistake, some readers may feel an impulse to dismiss the whole study as worthless. It will, however, be a good plan to examine the situation more coolly and consider in detail the exact respects in which Freud's arguments and conclusions are invalidated.

1. This was pointed out by Irma Richter in a footnote to her recently published selection from Leonardo's Notebooks (1952, 286). Like Pfister (p. 159*n.* below), she refers to Leonardo's childhood memory as a 'dream'.

In the first place the 'hidden bird' in Leonardo's picture (p. 159*n.*) must be abandoned. If it is a bird at all, it is a vulture; it bears no resemblance to a kite. This 'discovery', however, was not made by Freud but by Pfister. It was not introduced until the second edition of the work, and Freud received it with considerable reserve.

Next, and more important, comes the Egyptian connexion. The hieroglyph for the Egyptian word for 'mother' ('*mut*') quite certainly represents a vulture and not a kite. Gardiner in his authoritative *Egyptian Grammar* (2nd ed., 1950, 469) identifies the creature as '*Gyps fulvus*', the griffon vulture. It follows from this that Freud's theory that the bird of Leonardo's phantasy stood for his mother cannot claim direct support from the Egyptian myth, and that the question of his acquaintance with that myth ceases to be relevant.[1] The phantasy and the myth seem to have no immediate connexion with each other. Nevertheless each of them, taken independently, raises an interesting problem. How was it that the ancient Egyptians came to link up the ideas of 'vulture' and 'mother'? Does the egyptologists' explanation that it is merely a matter of a chance phonetic coincidence meet the question? If not, Freud's discussion of androgynous mother-goddesses must have a value of its own, irrespective of its connexion with the case of Leonardo. So too Leonardo's phantasy of the bird visiting him in his cradle and putting its tail into his mouth continues to cry out for an explanation even if the bird was not a vulture. And Freud's psychological analysis of the phantasy is not contradicted by this correction but merely deprived of one piece of corroborative support.

Apart, then, from the consequent irrelevance of the Egyptian discussion – though this nevertheless retains much of its independent value – the main body of Freud's study is unaffected by his mistake: the detailed construction of Leonardo's emotional life from his earliest years, the account of the conflict between his artistic and his scientific impulses, the deep analysis of his psychosexual history. And, in addition to this main topic, the study presents us with a number of not less important side-themes: a more general discussion of the nature and workings of the mind of the creative artist, an outline of the genesis of one particular

[1]. Nor can the story of the virginal impregnation of vultures serve as evidence of Leonardo's having had an exclusive bond with his mother in his infancy – though the existence of that bond is not contradicted by the failure of this particular evidence.

type of homosexuality, and – of special interest to the history of psycho-analytic theory – the first full emergence of the concept of narcissism.

This translation, by Alan Tyson, first appeared in 1957 in Volume XI of the Standard Edition of the Complete Psychological Works of Sigmund Freud. The present reprint is accompanied by a critical commentary by Mr Brian Farrell, Wilde Reader in Psychology in the University of Oxford. Mr Farrell is a distinguished academic psychologist and his comments will be received with interest and attention. Where, however, he proceeds beyond historical and aesthetic considerations to a more general criticism of Freud's views, it must be borne in mind that he is approaching the subject as a theoretician and philosopher without direct clinical knowledge of psycho-analysis. As a result, some of his views on the actual procedure of psycho-analysis would not be shared by those who have had practical psycho-analytic experience. Those, incidentally, who are anxious to look more deeply into the immediate topic of Freud's essay may be reminded of the recent publication of a detailed work on a large scale: *Leonardo da Vinci: Psychoanalytic Notes on the Enigma* by Dr K. R. Eissler.

JAMES STRACHEY

LIST OF ABBREVIATIONS

G.S. Freud, *Gesammelte Schriften* (12 vols.), Vienna, 1924–34.
G.W. Freud, *Gesammelte Werke* (18 vols.), London, from 1940.
C.P. Freud, *Collected Papers* (5 vols.), London, 1924–50.
Standard Ed. Freud, *The Standard Edition* (24 vols.), London, from 1953.

Square brackets indicate matter supplied by the editor.

BIBLIOGRAPHY

[*Trans.*: Peter and Alexis, London, 1950.]

MÜNTZ, E. (1899) *Léonard de Vinci*, Paris.

MUTHER, R. (1909) *Geschichte der Malerei* (3 vols.), Leipzig.

PATER, W. (1873) *Studies in the History of the Renaissance*, London.

PFISTER, O. (1913) 'Kryptolalie, Kryptographie und unbewusstes Vexierbild bei Normalen', *Jb. psychoan. psychopath. Forsch.*, **5**, 115.

REITLER, R. (1917) 'Eine anatomisch-künstlerische Fehlleistung Leonardos da Vinci', *Int. Z. Psychoan.*, **4**, 205.

RICHTER, I. A. (1952) *Selections from the Notebooks of Leonardo da Vinci*, London.

RICHTER, J. P. (1883) *The Literary Works of Leonardo da Vinci*, London (2nd ed., Oxford, 1939).

RÖMER, L. VON (1903) 'Über die androgynische Idee des Lebens', *Jb. sex. Zwischenst.*, **5**, 732.

ROSCHER, W. H. (1884–1937) *Ausführliches Lexikon der griechischen und römischen Mythologie*, Leipzig.

ROSENBERG, A. (1898) *Leonardo da Vinci*, Leipzig.

SADGER, I. (1908) *Konrad Ferdinand Meyer*, Wiesbaden.
  (1909) *Aus dem Liebesleben Nicolaus Lenaus*, Leipzig and Vienna.
  (1910) *Heinrich von Kleist*, Wiesbaden.

SCOGNAMIGLIO, N. (1900). See SMIRAGLIA SCOGNAMIGLIO, N. (1900).

SEIDLITZ, W. VON (1909) *Leonardo di Vinci, der Wendepunkt der Renaissance* (2 vols.), Berlin.

SMIRAGLIA SCOGNAMIGLIO, N. (1900) *Ricerche e documenti sulla giovinezza di Leonardo da Vinci (1452–82)*, Naples.

SOLMI, E. (1908) *Leonardo da Vinci* (German trans. by E. Hirschberg), Berlin.
  (1910) 'La resurrezione dell'opera di Leonardo', *Conferenze Fiorentine*, Milan, 1.

BIBLIOGRAPHY

VASARI, G. (1550) *Le vite de' più eccellenti architetti, pittori et scultori italiani*, Florence (2nd ed., 1568; ed. Poggi, Florence, 1919).

[*German Trans.: Leben der ausgezeichnetsten Maler, Bildhauer und Baumeister* (trans. L. Schorn), Stuttgart, 1843].

VOLD, J. MOURLY (1912) *Über den Traum* (2 vols.) (*German trans.* by O. Klemm), Leipzig.